The Art and Spirit
Of
Leadership

Judy Brown

Dreams
pg. 72

Permissions

From *Letters to Olga* by Vaclav Havel, translated by Paul Wilson, translation copyright 1984 by Rowahlt Taschenbuch Verlag, translation copyright 1988 by Paul Wilson, Copyright 1983 by Vaclav Havel. Used by permission of Alfred A. Knopf, a division of Random House Inc.

"The Woodcarver" by Thomas Merton from *The Way of Chuang Tzu*, copyright 1965 by The Abbey of Gethsemani. Reprinted by permission of New Directions Publishing Corp.

"*The Unicorn in the Garden*" by James Thurber copyright 1939 Conde Nast. All rights reserved. Originally published in *"The New Yorker"* October 21st 1939. Reprinted by permission.

Order this book online at www.trafford.com
or email orders@trafford.com

Most Trafford titles are also available at major online book retailers.

Printed in the United States of America.

ISBN: 978-1-4669-1048-5 (sc)
ISBN: 978-1-4669-1050-8 (hc)
ISBN: 978-1-4669-1049-2 (e)

Library of Congress Control Number: 2011963603

Trafford rev. 04/23/2013

 www.trafford.com

North America & International
toll-free: 1 888 232 4444 (USA & Canada)
phone: 250 383 6864 ♦ fax: 812 355 4082

Praise for *The Art and Spirit of Leadership*

"Judy Brown has done it again. Following on the heels of her highly acclaimed *A Leader's Guide to Reflective Practice*, Judy has named what we innately know about leadership, but oddly, seldom teach: The most powerful aspects of leadership emerge from the depths of spirit, imagination, grace, and mystery. This book is a rich contribution to our understanding of the inseparable realms of leadership and creative practices."

    Bonnie Allen, Director of Access to Justice Partnerships
    Mississippi Center for Justice

"I have a theory: there is a sweet spot where the science of leadership aligns with the most profound insights into human psychology and the most ancient of spiritual dimensions of working relationships—it is called the soul of leadership. Judy Brown knows where that sweet spot is like no one else I've ever worked with. Yes, she knows where the soul of leadership lives."

    Larry Minnix, President & CEO,
    Leading Age

"Judy Brown does the impossible in the *Art and Spirit of Leadership*: she offers hugely important information in a book that reads like a beautiful novel. I couldn't stop turning the pages! The elegant combination of research and skills with poetry and story offers both a reader's delight and a hugely practical resource."

    Sally Z. Hare, Ph. D., Singleton Distinguished Professor
    Emerita, Coastal Carolina University, and President, still
    learning, inc.

"Poetry, prose, principles and practices all woven together in a tapestry about leadership. The book is designed to connect to one part or another of a reader: the head, the heart, or the gut. No matter which, it is powerful."

    Roger Saillant Ph.D., Executive Director of The Fowler Center
    for Sustainable Value, Weatherhead School of Management,
    Case Western Reserve University.

"If you believe that deepening self-awareness and fostering creativity within ourselves and others are important ways we can grow as leaders, then you will find *The Art and Spirit of Leadership* a welcome companion on your journey too. This is a book not to be read so much as to be experienced, as Judy Sorum Brown takes us to places and among people with the skill of a poet and short-story writer. Read it with all your senses."

John Diffey, President and CEO,
The Kendal Corporation,

"A surprising book that lifts the spirit and engages both heart and mind. Every reader is sure to find at least a few of the twelve *Art and Spirit of Leadership* principles deeply resonant. The stories entertain, the poetry sings, while the leadership principles and practices guide us with a light, often humorous, touch. Judy Sorum Brown has written a work of wisdom that taps into dimensions of leadership typically absent in traditional management approaches."

Chris Laszlo, author, consultant, and Associate Professor
Case Western Reserve University

"It seems almost a paradox to call a life's work groundbreaking, but in this book, Judy Brown brings together thousands of hours of practice in both leadership development and poetry to produce something that is as surprising and eye-opening as it is logical and sound. Brown's practiced understanding of the creative process along with her deep appreciation for the nuanced and often mysterious dimensions of leadership combine to bring us a book that offers a fresh and important perspective on genuine leadership and inspiring management."

Dr. Michael S. Glaser, Poet Laureate of Maryland, 2004-2009

Gratitudes

Creating this book has been a joy, a pleasure. Alive. Full of surprises.

For their part in its creation, I appreciate

- Deb Higgins and Mark Nepo, my partners at the Fetzer Institute; and the Institute for its support for this project;

- Megan Scribner, my editor, who has the eye of an eagle, the touch of an artist, and the heart of a poet; and Leslie O'Leary for her neighborly stewardship of the details of copy editing;

- My wise colleagues and friends from three communities of practice with whom I have learned and shared so much— The Society for Organizational Learning, The Center for Courage and Renewal, and ALIA (Authentic Leadership in Action);

- The strangers who are no longer strangers, whose paths have criss-crossed with mine in this meandering journey of learning, creativity and spirit;

- Those who have inspired me—poets, practitioners, students, public leaders, people from all walks of life;

- My husband David for his steady stewardship and encouragement;

- My daughter Meg, for her role in continuing to expand my horizons. Thanks to her generation for carrying forward their own work of heart and spirit;

- My many partners, over the years, in this work of the heart;

$\wp$ The ancestors—those no longer with us—whose wisdom, guidance, presence and encouragement shine through these pages;

In these pages you are all present.
To each of you, my appreciation.

Judy Brown
2012

A Space for your Jottings

Your jottings

This symbol of a flame appears throughout the book, marking space where you can jot notes to yourself, create a dialogue with ideas in the book, record your own stories or poems—or just leave it as an open space.

Table of Contents

From "Sweet Gifts"

We finish circles
for each other,
stepping into stories
we don't know about,
renewing patterns
for ourselves and
sometimes for each other,
not even knowing
that we do it,
bringing simple gifts,
not guessing how
in doing so,
we draw a circle,
bringing back to life,
our own,
each others too,
sweet complicated things
with deep rich history,
long lost or just forgotten,
now recalled with puzzled smile,
accepted by our grateful hands,
our lives connected
by each other's
unexpected and sweet gifts.

Judy Brown, November 21, 2000

The Art and Spirit of Leadership
judybrown@aol.com   www.judysorumbrown.com

The Art and Spirit of Leadership

Introduction

The seeds of this book were planted years back, in a gathering of a dozen or so leadership scholars and practitioners interested in the relationship between the arts and leadership. We met for three days in a small Catholic retreat center outside Chicago, drawn together by the seeming incongruity between our work as leadership educators and the importance to all of us of our own artistic interests—one of us a torch singer, several of us poets, others musicians, painters, writers.

I know our dialogue was rich and provocative, but I can't remember a single word of it. What I remember vividly were moments of emotion, hilarity, surprise—where the creative and unexpected happened: one morning at breakfast the torch singer-scholar organized the women among us (including a Catholic nun) into a chorus-line to sing "Stand by your Man" to the wild applause of our male colleagues.

And at the other extreme of the unexpected were the surprises in the final moments of our gathering.

In those closing moments we were sitting in a circle, and someone to the left of me volunteered to begin our round-robin "check out" process. He spoke of the impact of our time together. As he and the others spoke, I realized that I had not a single word in mind to say when it came my turn. The only thing in my head was the words to the hymn "Amazing Grace," and my mind was not saying them. It was singing them. This was terrifying. I never sing in public. I have never sung in public. In fact, the main reason that I play the piano so well is so I can accompany others who sing in public. And then I don't have to sing!

The Art and Spirit of Leadership
judybrown@aol.com   www.judysorumbrown.com

One by one around the circle, each person in turn spoke of appreciation for the insights of our time together. The process moved inexorably towards me. Half-way around the circle, I got an iron grip on myself and recited over and over, "I will not sing 'Amazing Grace'." Then the colleague straight across from me began to speak slowly about the unexpected nature of art and creativity. I could feel my iron grip slipping as he spoke. Deliberately and thoughtfully, the check-out continued around the circle, past my poet friend Diane, who later said that by the time it was her turn, she had an odd sense that I was going to sing "Amazing Grace." And then to me.

I opened my mouth to say something, anything, and to my utter amazement, I began to sing "Amazing Grace." My colleagues seemed to take this in stride. I was stunned.

Then to close our time together, our colleague, who had guided us through the three days of dialogue, touched the button on the sound system. Unbeknownst to the rest of us, he had cued up a piece of music: it was a Native American pipe playing "Amazing Grace."

I returned home to the Washington DC area with this odd "Amazing Grace" experience in Chicago still on my mind. When Sunday came, I went to my Quaker Meeting. The Quaker practice is to sit in silence awaiting some possible message—perhaps just for oneself (as an unshared meditation) or perhaps to share with entire gathering (spoken briefly and modestly). Still, the only thing going on in my head was the song "Amazing Grace." Sung, not spoken. I now considered this quite a problem and was doing my level best to remain silent. We were rounding the time towards the close of the hour-long Meeting, and I'd managed a high level of self control and silence. But I was increasingly worried I would burst into song. Suddenly a young woman across the way stood to speak. "Thank Heavens," I thought, realizing there would be no time for other reflections after she finished. "Saved from singing in public!"

She told of having another driver cut her off in traffic. She said something rude in response, and her young son, from the back seat, said, "Mommy, send love." She told us how glad she was that Quaker practice taught our little children such ideas.
Then she paused. Took a breath. And began to sing "Amazing Grace." I was floored.

When Meeting was over, I crossed the room, introduced myself to the young woman and, after we exchanged pleasantries, asked, "Do you often sing in Meeting?" "No," she said, "Never. I have no idea where that came from."

Sometimes when the Universe wants us to pay attention, it sends repeated messages. I think "Amazing Grace" was one of them for me.

And it continues to be.

This week, as I've been writing, I have been looking out what we call our "Grace" window at home—so named because our friend Grace, who has a flair for design, suggested not just replacing the old window but cutting a much bigger hole so that a new larger window would frame the entire marshland to the south.

We did, and it created a view of the vast wilderness, a whole new world.

Last week, I called my brother to see how his mother-in-law is doing. She had been near death's door. This week she is up, out of the hospital and happily cruising with her walker, playing bridge again. Her name is Grace. "Amazing Grace," he says.

And yesterday, I went again to Quaker Meeting. It was a very quiet, peaceful meeting, only two messages in an hour. The first, a woman who speaks her gratitude for family, friends and the grace of God. The second, a man who stands later and says quietly, "Spirit isn't just what's inside us. It is what we share."

"Spirit isn't just what's inside us. It is what we share."

This seems to be at least part of the message of "Amazing Grace" – and many of my other experiences – that encouraged me to write this book, to share reflections somewhat off the beaten path of leadership, notions about spirit and art and their presence in the work of leadership.

 Your jottings

Leadership: From Science, To Art and Spirit

Notwithstanding the "Amazing Grace" experiences, most of my life has been spent as a leadership educator—in universities, in educational non-profit groups, in manufacturing plants, in retreats with engineers, artists and nurses, and in organizations helping work groups sort out dilemmas.

In each of these diverse settings, I have drawn on the scientific basis for leadership which comes from many fields: history, psychology, sociology, engineering, biology, neuroscience, management, ethics—to name a few. In fact, much of my work, particularly the graduate classes I have taught on "Leadership for the Public Good" has focused on the research-based guidance that comes to us from those fields.

Yet, as a leader, a leadership educator, and a poet, I have been particularly aware of the nuanced, ineffable and sometimes seemingly mysterious dimensions of leadership, including the role of presence, creativity, artistry, synchronicity and what we might call, for lack of a better word, the "spirit" of leadership.

Having spent years with the science of leadership, I now find myself drawn to exploring these more subtle dimensions. They seem to rest beyond the ken of today's science, although in years to come they may find support in emerging scientific findings.

We discover these dimensions through experience, but often find them hard to define or to put into words. That territory, where important things seem beyond words, while foreign to me as a leadership scientist and scholar, is natural territory to me as a poet.

The Art and Spirit of Leadership
judybrown@aol.com   www.judysorumbrown.com

Lead with the poetry

Lead
with the
poetry,
and let it grow
as it would want.
The soul
has longing
different
from the
wanting of the will—
it follows
different paths—
go with it.

Judy Brown, November 26, 2010

The Art and Spirit of Leadership
judybrown@aol.com   www.judysorumbrown.com

A wise colleague once reminded me that all good poems end in mystery. Perhaps here, musing about the more subtle dimensions of leadership—the practices of artistry, the worlds of creativity and spirit that are at the heart of creative leadership—perhaps here leadership is beyond theory, beyond technique and on terrain where some mystery will always remain.

And in such realms, we have a broader sense of leadership than is the norm, an understanding that leadership is not dependent on role or status. It is rather an orientation, a way of responding to life's challenges. Or, as one of my students noted, "It is a way of life." Here we see leadership as a moment-to-moment ethic of moving things ahead, of contributing to the common good. And here we have a sense that leadership, while historically thought of as an heroic, solo effort, is more often a matter of collective, collaborative energies over time.

In such a framing of leadership, much mystery remains. So perhaps the value of this writing is not only to offer some answers but to end with critical unanswered questions still before us. As Albert Einstein reminds us, "The most beautiful and profound emotion we can experience is the sensation of the mystical. It is the sower of all true science…to know what is impenetrable to us really exists, manifesting itself as the highest wisdom and the most radiant beauty."

The path of these musings is a path of spirit, not religion, and is an echo of Einstein's notion about the importance of knowing that what is "impenetrable to us really exists."

That awareness is at the heart of my leadership experience and my teaching, my learning and my life.

In courses I have developed on creative leadership and dialogue, as well as in my work helping organizations tap into a more dynamic and creative spirit, I have had many opportunities to be intentional about my own leadership practices, as well as to share leadership practices with others, and learn from their experiences. The work itself—teaching, coaching and leading—has been my "practice field" for these approaches.

What follows are my personal reflections on practices I believe can place us on the path of leading with art and spirit. My hope is that in the margins and white spaces of this book, you will find yourself remembering the practices that have sustained you, recalling practices of colleagues that have inspired you, and noting additional practices to support your leadership and your life.

A Stranger's Invitation, Leadership Practice and Principles

While I've long grappled with these ideas, the urge to write about them, to share them with you, was prompted by an unexpected encounter with a stranger and a surprising invitation. Perhaps most of our creative efforts are sparked by similar surprises— often prompted by strangers.

The Gift of Unexpected Encounters

It all came out of the blue. At the end of a speech I gave on the science of leading in tough times, a stranger approached me. He said he wanted me to be part of his organization's just-to-be launched leadership development program. I was intrigued by the nature of his invitation: "Others will be covering the science of leadership. We need you to share your perspectives on the art and spirit of leadership."

Startled, I asked what he had seen in my presentation that moved him to offer such an invitation. "I liked the way you wove ideas and poetry together, the way you organized ideas, and the delivery. Just do that for us."

Still puzzled, but with an instinctive sense that such an invitation was on my path in ways I couldn't yet understand, I flew to Connecticut to talk with a corporate group. The stranger who had approached me initially turned out to be the CEO, and his hope was that together we could strengthen the collective sense of the art and spirit of leadership.

I went because the very idea of such a conversation made my heart sing, and over the years I have learned to heed such signals from my heart. I travelled with a handwritten outline of twelve key ideas about leadership and a sheaf of poetry, mostly my own.

Those twelve ideas appear throughout this book as its chapter headings:

1) Listen to Yourself. Know What Makes Your Heart Sing

2) Pay Attention to Small, Early Signs Of The Presence Of the World You Long For

3) Model Humor, Humanity and Humility

4) Practice Generous, Wide Curiosity

5) Create Open Spaces for Yourself and For Others

6) Practice Creativity and Hold Onto The Powerful Images That Emerge From That Practice

7) Expect To Find Gems, Gifts and Genius In The Most Unexpected Packages

8) Take The Risk Of Being Less Than Perfect

9) Lead With Story and Invite Story From Others

The Art and Spirit of Leadership
judybrown@aol.com   www.judysorumbrown.com

10) Follow The Threads Of Aliveness

11) Risk Speaking In Your Natural Voice

12) Take Care Of Yourself; You Are A Treasure

While these twelve ideas are separate notions, in a larger sense they are interwoven in a patterned understanding of a way to live. Each is a part of a whole.

I am mindful that these notions about leading might as easily apply to teaching and learning – to life in general. These are principles and practices that enliven the space of learning as fully as they enliven organizations and movements. The link between leading and learning is evident in much of leadership thinking. Some of the most powerful leadership frameworks of our time (the work of Ron Heifetz at Harvard and Peter Senge at MIT, for instance) characterize the leader as, among other things, a teacher-learner, who creates conditions for learning and innovation and fosters a quality of dialogue leading to important break-throughs.

Living the twelve ideas into being

These twelve ideas or principles and the practices that make them evident are still growing, expanding, developing. They are emergent. Sharing them now, in this way, is in keeping with four of the twelve principles:

- Principle number six: "Practice creativity." This book is interspersed with my poetry. So my own creative practice is present in these pages.

- Principle number eight: "Risk being less than perfect." I am offering work that is evolving, in the process of becoming, writing with a sense that portions are still "under construction." I am sharing what is forming, with the hope it may be of worth to others and with the sure sense that it will help me learn what still needs to be understood and communicated. I hope you'll see this as an invitation to note your own thoughts, your stories and even your poetry.

- Principle number nine: "Lead with story." I have included many stories of leading and learning.

- Principle number eleven: "Risk speaking in one's own natural voice." The world often expects an educator to write in an objective voice, professionally, professorially. Yet here I write informally, personally, as if we were meeting over coffee to muse about the nuances of leadership, learning and life.

These twelve principles represent practices of the inner life—of the inner world of the learner and the leader. They turn our attention towards our inner life as the foundation of the life-affirming transformation we hope for in the outer world. That link reminds us that our efforts to attend to our inner state are important to the state of the world. Our disciplined attention to our inner life matters to those around us, as well as to those we lead. As Vaclav Havel notes in his poem "It is I who must Begin,"

> Whether all is really lost
> or not depends entirely on
> whether or not I am lost.

When we are, to use Havel's words, "not ... lost," we have the chance to lead with a presence and wholeness which frees others to act more fully, more confidently. Such presence, wholeness and authenticity grow from a discipline touching both our inner life and our life in the world.

The Art and Spirit of Leadership
judybrown@aol.com   www.judysorumbrown.com

It was Havel, the oft-imprisoned dissident and world-renowned poet, who led Czechoslovakia through a peaceful revolution to independence in 1989. He later served as his country's first president. In 2009 he spoke of leadership in his welcome to the International Leadership Association conference in Prague. He noted that in the course of the "Velvet Revolution," which was headquartered in Prague twenty years earlier, he had come to an important understanding about his own role. He realized that people needed him to be present, not because there was anything only he could do, but rather because he had come to represent to them a presence that allowed them to "take action without being confused."

Havel's thoughts about leadership (and his reluctance to characterize himself as a leader) are a provocative challenge: *Self-discovery* We, as leaders, must know ourselves, so we are not lost. We must know the inner terrain from which we lead as surely as we know the outer world in which we lead. It is that awareness that gives us hope of being able to be a presence enabling others to take action. *Self-knowledge*

The Paradox Of Connecting And Letting Go

And in varying, often indirect ways, the twelve ideas that form this book touch on two paradoxical energies: on the one hand, connecting and on the other hand, letting go. These two paradoxical energies seem to me parallel to, or akin to, love and forgiveness. Love is the energy of connection and unity. Forgiveness is the energy of setting aside, letting go, walking past.

Many of these twelve practices create or uncover connection, a sense of oneness, what one person in a recent dialogue experience called "unity." Others are practices that allow us to let go, to set aside, to move beyond—in a sense to forgive ourselves and one another for imperfection, for not being who or what we want, for disappointments, for deep hurts.

Each practice taps into a special kind of dynamic that lies at the heart of what it takes to be alive to the world around us, just as it is, and to use our attention and our energy in ways that are healthy and constructive, fostering the world we wish to create.

In simultaneously holding these two dynamics of connecting and of letting go, we are more likely to create a space of potential, of possibility, of giftedness, of grace—what Otto Scharmer and his colleagues in writing about "presencing" term a space of "letting come." Or what my friend, researcher Marcial Losada, calls "possibility space." A space of enormous innovation, creativity and energy.

The Power of Practice

Practice means trial & error not perfection

What I once shared with the strangers in Connecticut, who are no longer strangers, was my sense that creative leadership, artistry and spirit grow out of practice—practice akin to that of an athlete or a musician—repeated, daily practice. These leadership practices are similar to the practice of a landscape painter, or a great pianist-composer, or a fine photographer. It seems to me the great painter is great because she paints canvas after canvas. The composer, composes—first one piece, then another and another. The great photographer takes thousands and thousands of pictures. The poet (and here I can speak from personal experience) plays with words at every chance she gets.

The gift grows more powerful because of the inner passion for the field, for the art. That passion fuels energy for relentless, ongoing practice. The gift grows with the joy of fiddling with sounds, experimenting with images, playing with words and surfaces and light.

The notion of the importance of practice in any field, including leadership, is central to a growing field of inquiry about the role of practice and discipline in turning whatever level of raw talent and

23   The Art and Spirit of Leadership
judybrown@aol.com   www.judysorumbrown.com

interest one may possess into a noteworthy contribution. I have been intrigued by these ideas as they are developed in Malcolm Gladwell's book, *Outliers*. Gladwell notes the common pattern among the leaders in their fields (those who are highly successful in fields from hockey to music to business) : they feel such passion about their work that they expend at least 10,000 hours in practice.

Ten Thousand Hours of Practice???

At first, my reaction to the idea of 10,000 hours of practice was that "mere mortals" can't do that much practicing. Fine for hockey players, but not likely for me. Then I began to ask myself what would be the component practices of my own leadership work. I listed some: journaling to get focused and centered before the day begins; creating alive conversations and listening with full focus; asking completely open questions; helping people identify their own talents and gifts. Before long, I had a fairly long list of regular practices. But 10,000 hours? Impossible.

So I did the math on just one item: my 30 minute, early-morning journal work. This practice gives me a chance to reflect on the day before, to take stock of what matters no matter what lies ahead and to be present to the aliveness of the moment of writing. And that's where almost all of my poetry shows up. I carefully noted the exact number of years I'd faithfully, doggedly maintained my half-hour a day journal practice. Twenty nine years. Every day. That worked out to 5,292.5 hours of practice before I actually "did" anything, before my day officially begins with its natural practice of conversations, listening, problem-solving and decision-making. So perhaps the 10,000 hours of practice is more possible than we realize.

A friend pointed out that my own disciplined practice—not just the journaling, but other practices as well—enabled me to accept the invitation from the stranger to speak on the art and spirit of leadership, to step into the space and possibility that our connection in that moment created.

What Is Practice In Leadership?

What is "practice" in the world of leadership? Practice as we are exploring it here operates in three distinct ways, three different dimensions.

curious

- First, there are things we do, the ways we carry out our leadership, that are our "practices." For instance, for me, the intentional act of stepping toward conflict in a constructive, inquiring way is a practice. It does not come naturally. I don't like conflict. I grew up in a conflict-averse culture, but I have practiced daily over the years, stepping toward conflict, engaging constructively and asking open questions. That is my "practice."

cohort groups

- Second, I have been part of "communities of practice" – organizations, movements, groups of colleagues—that hold to certain practices or sets of practices. Being part of these communities of practice helps me strengthen my capacities as a leader. For instance, my ability to notice and counter my internal aversion to conflict has been strengthened by what I have learned in the community known as "Authentic Leadership in Action," which is a group of colleagues for whom meditation is a foundational practice. My capacity to ask open and curious questions has been strengthened by my participation in the community of practice known as "Courage and Renewal" organized around the work of Parker Palmer. My capacity to lead and learn simultaneously has been strengthened by my participation in the Society for Organizational Learning, organized around the work of Peter Senge and colleagues at MIT.

- Third is the role of "practice fields." If we pay attention, we can see that life presents us with "practice fields" — circumstances where we can use our practice to good end. Sometimes our reaction to the presence of the "practice field" is not a happy one: "Oh, rats, not another one of these difficult conflicts!!!" But these practice fields are important opportunities for growing our skills by using them on the spot. So, for instance, when I am working with a group on dialogue skills, and someone comes at me aggressively with, "This is all fine and good, but we don't have time for these long drawn out dialogues. They are just time wasters. We have important work to do." Instead of running for cover or the exit (as is my natural tendency), I take a breath, note to myself that this is a "practice field," and ask an open question, perhaps, "When have you had a conversation that seemed sort of long-ish at the time, but that saved you a lot of time later, and made it easier to get the work done?"

put it into action

In the world of leadership, the notion of practice operates in several dimensions at once – our individual practices, communities of practice, and practice fields. It is a pattern that "scales" in the sense of the science of "chaos," where scaling means that a pattern shows up at many levels.

Lessons From Other Practice Fields

I have learned the most about "lifetime" practice from fields quite different from mine. From athletics. From music. From crafts. And from the headlines in the newspaper.

One of my all-time favorite headlines about the power of passion and practice is the story of a commercial airline pilot. In January 2009, US Air Captain Sullenberger managed to land a commercial jet with all its engines shut down and 155 passengers and crew on board on the Hudson River without any loss of life. How does a

The Art and Spirit of Leadership
judybrown@aol.com   www.judysorumbrown.com

person manage that, we might ask. The answer lies in a life-time of practice—that comes together in an unexpected "practice field."

Chessie Sullenberger's love of flying drew him (or drove him) from teen years on to become an expert on all forms of aircraft. Fascinated with flying, Sullenberger attended the Air Force Academy where, even as a student, he quickly became their expert on piloting gliders. Over the years, first in the military and later as a commercial pilot, he flew all manner of aircraft, served as a check-pilot, a safety expert, and studied crash landings— particularly on water. He loved flying, and his curiosity about it seemed boundless.

After decades of practicing his craft, he found himself at the controls of a totally silent commercial airliner, with a full complement of passengers and crew, floating about 3000 feet over the city of New York. Its powerful engines had completely shut down after having sucked in a flock of geese. He reported later that the first thing he noticed was that the aircraft's windshield was covered with geese. Then he noticed the engines were silent. Then he noticed the smell of cooked goose.

In the three minutes from the time the engines stopped until he set that plane down on the Hudson River, Captain Sullenberger managed the seemingly impossible. Explaining to the air traffic controller guiding him that he didn't have enough lift to make it to any of the area airports, he said calmly, "We'll be on the Hudson," and then safely landed his aircraft on the Hudson River on a cold day in January.

So smoothly did he set the silent plane down on the water that the flight attendants sitting in the jump-seat just behind the cockpit thought they had landed on a runway. Everything about the landing was marked by practices of calm and discipline. The calm in the cockpit as they floated above the city (Sullenberger to his longtime colleague and copilot: "Any ideas?" "No, not really.")

27

The calm after the plane came to a rest on the river. In unison the two men said to each other, "That wasn't so bad."

Had he been worried about the crew and the passengers? No. He knew he had a skilled cabin crew and trusted completely in their ability to do their job, to prepare the passengers for landing. He could hear their voices from behind the cockpit door: "Brace. Head down. Stay down."

He said he had only three things to pay attention to: airspeed, altitude, and keeping the wings absolutely level. He remembered two additional things from having studied landings on water (usually referred to as crashes): the value of putting the plane down near rescue boats (he noticed that there were ferries on either side of the river where he was headed) and the importance of the precise angle of the body of the plane as it touched down on water. He knew the math of that angle.

As the passengers were standing on the wings and climbing aboard the ferries which had headed immediately toward the floating plane, Captain Sullenberger double-checked the cabin to be sure everyone was out. As soon as he was out of the aircraft, he repeatedly checked the passenger manifest to make sure everyone was accounted for—all evidence of a lifetime of practice as a pilot and captain.

Later, when his home town insisted on honoring him for the heroism he denied was heroism, his only words to the community members gathered: "Thank you. I had a great team."

Practice hones our focus and frees us from distractions. It allows us to step into a challenge with equanimity or, as Vaclav Havel would say, "without being confused." Too often when we begin important work, we are deluged with distractions and anxieties. We become confused. That's human. Yet it is the inner practices which can clear away the confusion. While Sullenberger's story is a contemporary one of life and death, not all of our challenges are life and death. But the wisdom holds true.

We find that wisdom as well in a much older story from another culture, offering parallel guidance about practice and its impact on our ability to meet a challenge: The six-thousand year old story of the woodcarver from Thomas Merton's translation of *The Way of Chuang Tzu*, is also a story of practice, focus, care and attention. In that legend, a craftsman sets aside the praise that suggests the beautiful bell stand he has carved is magic, "the work of the spirits," and instead explains the practices, mostly inner and mostly in advance of the actual work, that allow him the focused attention to do what is needed. To step into, what he characterizes as a "live encounter."

The woodcarver tells the Prince and the assembled crowd of his way of taking time to prepare himself for the work:

The Woodcarver

Khing, the master carver, made a bell stand
Of precious wood. When it was finished,
All who saw it were astounded. They said it must be
The work of spirits.
The Prince of Lu said to the master carver:
"What is your secret?"
Khing replied: "I am only a workman:
I have no secret. There is only this:
When I began to think about the work you commanded
I guarded my spirit, did not expend it
On trifles, that were not to the point.
I fasted in order to set
My heart at rest.
After three days fasting,
I had forgotten gain and success.

The Art and Spirit of Leadership
judybrown@aol.com   www.judysorumbrown.com

After five days
I had forgotten praise or criticism.
After seven days
I had forgotten my body
With all its limbs.

By this time all thought of your Highness
And of the court had faded away.
All that might distract me from the work
Had vanished.
I was collected in the single thought
Of the bell stand.

Then I went to the forest
To see the trees in their own natural state.
When the right tree appeared before my eyes,
The bell stand also appeared in it, clearly, beyond doubt.
All I had to do was to put forth my hand
and begin.

If I had not met this particular tree
There would have been
No bell stand at all.

What happened?
My own collected thought
Encountered the hidden potential in the wood;
From this live encounter came the work
Which you ascribe to the spirits."

These words stay with me, ringing in my ears. "By this time....all that might distract me from the work had vanished. I was collected in the single thought of the bell stand....From this live encounter came the work which you ascribe to the spirits."

The practices that allow us to be collected, to collect ourselves, in such a way that we can step into a live encounter without being beset by distractions, confusion, anxiety—these are at the heart of leadership, learning and life.

Whether we take guidance from the miracle on the Hudson splashed across the headlines in *The New York Times* or from the poem of the Woodcarver in classic Chinese literature thousands of years old, we are well served to think of the power of practice, and of the power that inner practices can give us to set aside all that might distract us from our work and to be present to the live encounters that life offers us.

Sullenberger's landing and the woodcarver's remarkable work are both "miracles" that emerge from a life-time of disciplined practice.

What Are Our Ten Thousand Hours Of Leadership Practice?

The research, Gladwell's *Outliers*, Captain Sullenberger's remarkable landing on the Hudson River and story of the Woodcarver's beautiful bell stand raise the same question: What are the 10,000 hours of practice that place us on the path of spirited and creative leadership?

The answer must be very personal and individual. And yet I think we can learn with and from each other about those practices.

The Art and Spirit of Leadership
judybrown@aol.com   www.judysorumbrown.com

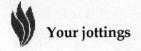 **Your jottings**

The Art and Spirit of Leadership
judybrown@aol.com   www.judysorumbrown.com

Stay centered

Stay centered.
It is your greatest gift
to the world,
to those
you care about,
to your own soul,
in fact.
Whatever is required
for you to stay completely
centered in your gifts—
to listen
to the silence
of the greater universe—
do that thing now,
this very moment.

Judy Brown, November 3, 2006

The Art and Spirit of Leadership
judybrown@aol.com   www.judysorumbrown.com

But first, let us remember the twelve principles of the art and spirit of leadership, those that emerged for me in response to the invitation from the stranger, each of which serves as the heading of a chapter to follow.

The Art and Spirit of Leadership Principles

1) Listen To Yourself. Know What Makes Your Heart Sing

2) Pay Attention To Small, Early Signs Of The Presence Of The World You Long For

3) Model Humor, Humanity and Humility

4) Practice Generous, Wide Curiosity

5) Create Open Spaces For Yourself and For Others

6) Practice Creativity and Hold Onto The Powerful Images That Emerge From That Practice

7) Expect To Find Gems, Gifts and Genius In The Most Unexpected Packages

8) Take The Risk Of Being Less Than Perfect

9) Lead With Story and Invite Story From Others

10) Follow The Threads Of Aliveness

11) Risk Speaking In Your Natural Voice

12) Take Care Of Yourself; You Are A Treasure

Chapter One

Listen To Yourself.
Know What Makes Your Heart Sing

Listen to your true self, to the inner voice that speaks of what matters most to you. Too often in our efforts to be responsive to the world around us, to take action, to get the work out the door, we grow deaf to our inner voice. We lose the ability to sense what makes our heart sing and alternatively what makes our heart sink. Listening to our inner sense of things is critical to leadership that is grounded in presence, integrity and authenticity.

We might think that listening to our heart's song is somehow selfish, not reflective of our commitments to the world and the needs of others. Or, that it will distract us from the practical requirements of life. And yet it is the surest guide to a calling that is our own, to a path that will tap our energies and talents. And one that will, in turn, contribute the most to the world.

For me, my heart songs often show up as poetry. And, though they sing true enough to me, I don't expect that they will necessarily have equal resonance for others. So I've been startled that when I share my poetry, which at times seems to me frivolous and personal standing next to the shared miseries in the world, people go out of their way to let me know how it has helped them. And to my great surprise, how it has helped them in very practical ways.

Perhaps my most telling experience was when the Governor of Maryland was interviewed about leading in tough times and quoted my poem "Trough" saying that it gave voice to his experience of trying to govern.

Trough

There is a trough in waves,
a low spot
where horizon disappears
and only sky
and water
are our company.

And there we lose our way
unless
we rest, knowing the wave will bring us
to its crest again.

There we may drown
if we let fear
hold us within its grip and shake us
side to side,
and leave us flailing, torn, disoriented.

But if we rest there
in the trough,
are silent,
being with
the low part of the wave,
keeping
our energy and
noticing the shape of things,
the flow,

then time alone
will bring us to another
place
where we can see
horizon, see the land again,
regain our sense
of where
we are,
and where we need to swim.

Judy Brown, January 21, 1996

The Art and Spirit of Leadership
judybrown@aol.com www.judysorumbrown.com

Our heart songs offer powerful guidance about the path upon which our soul longs to travel, and upon which our feet will be most sure. And often they appear as a subtle yearning for something elusive and hard to define.

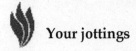 **Your jottings**

Trust the tug of yearning

Trust the tug
of yearning.
Let your heart
follow
what it
most loves.
Longing
is a powerful
compass.
It will always
bring you home,
although the road
may sometimes
be a rough one.

Judy Brown, July 25, 2009

The Art and Spirit of Leadership
judybrown@aol.com www.judysorumbrown.com

A colleague who leads a federal program asked permission to send this poem about yearnings to his daughter. Somehow he thinks she should see it. His own longing, one that has shaped his years of leadership in environmental stewardship, his honest reporting about the pressures and encroachment of development on our unspoiled landscapes, and his commitment to wise and beautiful community design was formed in the crucible of the loss of the landscape in which he grew up to the forces of economic development in Northern Virginia. He knows firsthand about the "tug of yearning" and about the road that is often a rough one.

Perhaps that's why he wanted his daughter to have the poem. Even early in life, overwhelmed by the demands of adult life that lie ahead, it is easy for our young people to lose sight of their dreams, of what makes their heart sing. I remember from my early years as an academic dean, the students who would come in and explain their plans to me:

> "I plan to get a degree in accounting because I know there will be jobs for accountants."
>
> Gently, I would ask: "Do you know what it's like to be an accountant?"
>
> The answer, invariably: "No, not really."
>
> Second question: "Given what you imagine the work is like, do you think you would enjoy it?"
>
> The answer: "No not really, but I know I can get a job."
>
> "What do you really love to do?" Their answers to that question would light up the student, and my office.

The Art and Spirit of Leadership
judybrown@aol.com www.judysorumbrown.com

"But there aren't many jobs in that," the student would say.

Even as a practical person attuned to the everyday realities of work and putting food on the table, I never could wrap my mind around plotting paths that gave students a 100% chance of getting jobs they didn't really want rather than a lesser chance of working at something they loved.

In these dialogues with students about their plans and dreams, I could see how challenging it is to find one's way in the world and also stay attuned to what makes one's heart sing. And I could identify with the challenge of knowing what makes your heart sing, and the implications of living with the knowledge.

I appreciated the temptation to simply not acknowledge, not even discover, what makes our heart sing. But knowing needn't throw our lives into a "cocked hat" as they say in the Midwest.

Awareness is awareness; it is not a command.

For many of us, what makes our heart sing may change as the seasons of our life change. So staying attuned to our heart and its signals requires a lifetime of the ongoing practice of attentiveness. A friend said to me that for her, the early signals are less a "song" than a "warming," so she has begun a journal to keep track of what "warms her heart."

For some of us, our heart song will find its way as an avocation, a sideline, at least for much of our life. But awareness of it and honoring it with time and practice, keeps it alive, and allows it to inform all we do. That is the story I would tell of my poetry, which first emerged in the pages of my journal, and of its place in my life and my work.

The Art and Spirit of Leadership
judybrown@aol.com www.judysorumbrown.com

Why the journal?

Why the journal?
To sit with something
of yourself,
as you would
sit in church,
or with
a tearful child.

Why the journal now?
To notice questions
that are threads
in webs of life
we often move too fast to see.

Why the journal?
To be whole.

Judy Brown, November 17, 2006

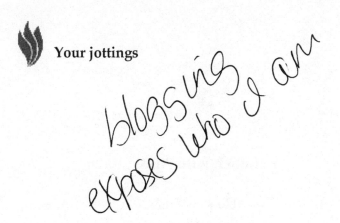

Your jottings

blogging exposes who I am

Why take notes? Because it's easy to miss the signals. It's tempting, often second nature, to remain committed to something that made our heart sing years ago, without noticing that the heart has begun writing a new song. And particularly if the emerging heart song seems to lead us on a new path, our fears and longings for predictability may keep us doggedly following the same old tune.

But life brings us changes, and often they begin within. Sometimes the early excitement of achievement or competition gives way to other joys. That's what I could see in the life of a colleague and friend of mine whose words to the Dean of our Public Policy School prompted a poem.

Lunch with Alice

He's leaving
the academy,
he told the Dean.

It seems
he wants
to linger longer
over lunch
with Alice,
his beloved.

World-renowned
for his intellect,
the Nobel prize in hand,
he's listening
to his heart.

Judy Brown May 25, 2003

It's possible in mid-life, or later, to be awakened to a new sense of calling surprisingly unlike that which drew us earlier. I am thinking of the choice of a Wall Street financier who recently left New York to lead a Quaker school in the community in which he grew up. "Where else can you wear Croc's (the brightly colored, rubber garden shoes) to work?" he asks with pleasure. And with the sense of being where he is supposed to be at this time in his life.

Knowing who we are at heart, not only provides us with critical guidance about our path, but it also increases our curiosity about who the "other" is, at heart. If we are hardened against listening to our own true nature, we will be hardened to the subtle signs of who the other is.

Self - coaching TDL Models

But when we can explore that knowing in ourselves and encourage it in others, both by example and inquiry, we unleash a depth of bright energy otherwise submerged by the layers of life that press it out of sight.

Nonetheless staying thus attuned can be difficult in a world that may seem to value qualities other than those at the core of who we are. We ourselves, distracted by the signals from that world, may long for gifts that are not our own, seeking jobs and achievements that overlook our greatest gifts.

In my own efforts to maneuver those crosscurrents, the practice of writing poetry has provided the greatest guidance. The practice of noticing the words that poke their heads up into my consciousness, and jotting them down without a need to understand where they are going, is a practice of staying in touch with the "me" that is outside (or perhaps better put, deeper inside) my dogged discipline and direction. It gives me a way to sense into the gifts of life I could easily overlook.

The Art and Spirit of Leadership
judybrown@aol.com www.judysorumbrown.com

Sands

Writing poetry
is the practice
of seeing in stillness,
listening for silence
that has wonder
underneath it,
holding the grains
of gratitude
that remain after the
whispered wave
of the moment
recedes to the sea.

Judy Brown, January 15, 2007

The Art and Spirit of Leadership
judybrown@aol.com www.judysorumbrown.com

This lesson of staying attuned to the inner dimensions of our true nature, and that of others, came to me most powerfully from an experience with a student. I think of this as "Caroline's story," but perhaps it is also my story.

A few years back, I was particularly aware of "being a softie" (as my law-school student daughter calls me) in a world that wants hard edges, clear rules and toughness. I had just received a note sent to faculty reminding us it was important to the reputation of our highly competitive graduate programs that we be tough on grades and class attendance. So after a lifetime of chastising myself for being a softie, I took a breath, and decided it was time to step up to being appropriately tough. After all, being a faculty member demanded certain things of me!

So I launched my graduate leadership class by reminding everyone that our class would meet for seven full days over the semester and that everyone should expect to be present for all seven days. No excuses. Despite what seemed like undue toughness on my part, the first class went well.

We began our second class session with a check-in, round robin, and when it came Caroline's turn (Caroline was a quiet, understated, Air Force Academy graduate headed eventually for fighter-pilot training), she said she had a dilemma. She'd been asked to represent the Air Force as their runner in an important race against the other armed services. She wasn't really a runner, she said. But she'd been running lately and liked it. And she would only compete if I said it was OK to miss class to run the race, because as Murphy's Law of class attendance would have it, the race was scheduled for the third of our seven class meetings.

I had this strange feeling of being tested in some way, but I wasn't sure what the test was. All eyes were on me as I sat with Caroline, and her dilemma, quickly becoming my dilemma as well. I found myself saying, "Well, Caroline, I realize the Air Force wants you

47

The Art and Spirit of Leadership
judybrown@aol.com www.judysorumbrown.com

to run this race, but I'm curious: Do you yourself really want to run it?" Her eyes lit up. "Yes," was her quiet answer.

Later I recalled the symphony conductor Ben Zander saying that the test of a leader is whether folks in the organization have shining eyes. Caroline's eyes were shining when she said "Yes." But at that moment, with that circle of students, I had only the sense that there was much more to Caroline than a public policy student sitting before me with a dilemma, and I was much more than a faculty member trying to maintain discipline. Time stood still.

shining eyes

"OK, Caroline," I said, "I think you should go run the race. And send us all an e-mail about the leadership lessons you uncover in this experience." Caroline won that race. And because she did, the joint US Armed Forces asked her to compete for all the Armed Forces in a race just days ahead in Europe (she'd never been out of the US). She also won that one. By the time she returned for our fourth session (having sent her required e-mails about leadership lessons from the races), this quiet, self-described "non-runner" had successfully run two important races.

That day, that moment, when I bent my own world-imposed rule because of the look in her eyes, has stayed with me.

This year one of my current students, also an Air Force Academy graduate, said, "Did you hear what happened to Caroline?" It turned out there was more to the story. Caroline graduated from our Masters program and was headed for Air Force flight training, when she found out that there was a marathon in Minneapolis that would put her on the path to the next Olympic tryouts. She convinced the Air Force to let her put off the start of flight training, and she ran the race and made the cut. Her e-mail to friends at school includes a photo of her standing, glowing, with her family, at the finish-line.

Whether Caroline makes it to the Olympics or does not, I hop
have learned that the person across from me is much, much m
than whatever role the world and I have assigned them. And t
the same is true of me. We owe it to each other to allow ourselves
a wholeness that the world may neither perceive, nor encourage.
The world we dream of lies in that spaciousness. It is the space of
knowing what makes the heart sing.

And, should we think the question of what makes our heart sing
seems too "touchy-feely" for the hard-working executive, I
remember with pleasure my experience at the University of Texas
at San Antonio, with my colleague Bob Lengel, economist and
engineer, who heads the Business School's Center for Professional
Excellence there.

Bob designs and leads programs for mid-career executives and
leads those executives through an exercise which he calls
"spirit/no spirit."

In a straightforward manner, he asks very practical people where
in their work they have a sense of "spirit" and where the spirit is
completely gone—conditions which he names "no spirit." All he
has to do is pose that question, frame that contrast, and the room
comes immediately alive with examples. No need for fancy
definitions, no worry about the conversation being too "touchy-
feely" or too spiritual. The tough, seasoned executives
understand the question immediately and they are in the
conversation with all of themselves. "Spirit. No spirit." The
contrast is clear. So, too, for most of us, if we allow ourselves to
think about it.

Thinking about spirit and no spirit, thinking about our deepest
questions often requires solitude and knowing ourselves. We are
kept so busy with the work of the world, that it takes
determination and practice to do the inner work that allows us to
do the outer work wisely and well. My colleague Bob also

49

reminds us of the wisdom found in one of the classics of science fiction, that the way to enslave a people is to keep them busy and take away their front porches.

One of life's surprises: After Bob led us through a four-week executive program for a highly respected local corporation, the firm's leadership decided to present classic rocking chairs as graduation gifts. Not only for the corporate folks, but also for those of us who were faculty. The rocking chair sits on the porch of my family home in Michigan, as a reminder of that learning community and that when we forget the porches and the rockers, we begin to enslave ourselves.

I have been writing these past few days standing at an architect's table –it's easier on my back—in the living room, near the piano. Every half hour or so, I stop writing and shift gears—usually sitting down at the piano and playing a song or two. I just wrote the words about solitude, and feeling somewhat tired, I sat down and opened the Quaker hymnal to a random page. It said: "Blessed quietness, holy quietness, what assurance in my soul! On the stormy sea, speaking peace to me, how the billows cease to roll." I appreciate the reminder and the synchronicity. "Blessed quietness….how the billows cease to roll."

The Art and Spirit of Leadership
judybrown@aol.com www.judysorumbrown.com

Chapter Two

Pay Attention To Small, Early Signs
Of The Presence Of The World You Long For

An incoming e-mail has a tag line that stops me in my tracks: "The future is already present; it's just unequally distributed." Our task then, as leaders and teachers, is to be awake to the small and early signs of the future, unequally distributed as it is. We need to be awake to any signs of the future we want to create, the future we long for, which is, given the unequal distribution, sometimes in short supply around us. But unlikely to be totally absent.

For me, the future we would create would be more generous, more thoughtful, and more caring, and less competitive, less cut-throat, less driven. You probably have your own words for it. But the key is to watch for the tiny seeds of that new world, and pay attention to them.

A world of generosity

Plant seeds for your future

My most unshakeable experience with that future, with that world in its "seed state," came unexpectedly in the very challenging and trying time when my daughter Meg was applying to law school. In the summer following her senior year at college, Meg, after pleasantly surprising herself at how well she had done on the LSAT, had been accepted at a number of fine law schools, the strongest of which was Georgetown in Washington, DC.

But her dream school, in her dream city of New York, remained elusive. NYU Law School had placed her on a waitlist and showed no signs of giving her a seat in their late August class. Georgetown was a fine school, nationally respected, but Meg had grown up in the DC area and had gone to high school in DC.

The Art and Spirit of Leadership
judybrown@aol.com   www.judysorumbrown.com

Georgetown felt like coming back home for law school, and besides, she dreamed of New York. But July came and went and still no news from NYU.

So, with our help, Meg, decided that she needed to get herself organized to go to Georgetown. Together we found her a lovely and tiny apartment near DuPont Circle, in DC. It was her first place on her own—a big step.

The leasing agent was named Brian—a good-spirited, helpful young man. He arranged to have the apartment painted and fixed up. Meg's step-dad built her a dresser that would fit in the closet. We helped her move her beloved desk chair, mattress, bedding, a few pots and pans and dishes into the apartment, imagining that on weekends when she visited friends in NYC, we might borrow her "city pad" and see what it would be like to move in from the suburbs and live down by "hip" DuPont Circle.

It was an exciting time, but always a little bittersweet because of her disappointment about NYU. Over the few weeks of finding the apartment and moving Meg in, we got to know our leasing agent, Brian, pretty well. There was a wonderful generosity of spirit about him, a way of connecting with us. And we shared with him that NYU Law School was really Meg's dream school, but it hadn't come through. That she remained on the wait list. We also told him how much we loved her beautiful little apartment and appreciated the way he'd fixed it up.

After her first night in her own place, our phone rang in the morning. It was Meg. We asked how she'd enjoyed her "new home." "Loved it," she said. And, "Guess what!" NYU Law School had just contacted her and offered her a seat in the class that would start in three weeks.

What in the world could we do? We were responsible for the apartment in DC and knew that one in New York would be even more costly. And as she said, "We certainly can't afford two apartments."

We would have to tell Brian our dilemma. "Mom, will you talk to him?" In a moment of Mother-weakness, I said yes. What in the world would I say? Dilemmas that are a mix of love and money are always hard for me. They bring out my most un-centered, unsettled self.

So I did what I often do in such unsettled circumstances: I began writing e-mails to myself of what I would say to Brian about Meg getting into NYU Law. The first e-mail fairly reeked of my panic, my wanting Meg to have what she wanted, my knowing they had us over a barrel about the apartment and that there was nothing I could do about it. That awful "stuck" feeling. But by the time I got to "practice e-mail" numbers three and four, I'd pretty well written myself past my panic, past my desperation and into a space of relative calm, of hopeful dreams, and helping hands. A very different emotional space. One that fairly reflected the experience we'd had with Brian from the start. By the time I'd done the sixth practice e-mail (yes, it really took that many), I was really feeling hopeful and excited about what had happened for Meg. And appreciative of Brian's help so far.

Then I called Brian. "Brian, this is Judy Brown, Meg's Mom. Remember when I said Meg was waitlisted by NYU Law School?" There was a long moment of silence on the phone. "Did they let her in?" asked Brian quietly. "Yes," I responded haltingly. Another long silence. And then Brian, with true excitement said, "Oh, and that's her dream school, isn't it? What wonderful news." "Yes," I said. "It is her dream school."

"Well, we certainly wouldn't want to stand in the way of her going to her dream school," he said, without missing a beat. We talked a bit longer, and the two of us agreed it would be fair if we paid a month's rent, as he'd painted the place, and she had already moved in.

When I relayed the phone conversation to Meg, she said through her tears, in semi-disbelief, "Are they running a business down there or what?" I would say now that they were running a new world, creating the world we dream of. Bit by bit. And whenever we see that happen, we need to note it and remember, so when the chance comes, we can remind ourselves to create a bit more of it for others.

The power of noticing

If we are quiet, and aware, we can see the small signs of the better world that we are working to create, that we want to help create. By noticing those small signs, by placing our attention on them, we amplify them. We fan those flames with our attention.

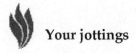 **Your jottings**

Sometimes this approach requires nothing more complicated than noticing small kindnesses, unexpected generosities. Subtle caring. Taking note of what seems unusual, yet life-affirming. I found such an experience in a cab ride to the San Antonio Airport:

For Leon
Whose name was on the taxi receipt

"I didn't plan
to drive a cab,"
he said.
"My business folded—
dry wall—
big homes—
but I'm enjoying this—
the independence—
working when I want."

I'd asked about
the limestone rock,
(six inches thick
and big, heavy)
he had inside the
van door.

"It's for the elders,"
he explained,
"They need a
step up to get in—
So I carry
this rock—
those flimsy plastic
steps aren't safe.

I tell
them it's my tombstone,"
he says laughing.
"It's a steppingstone."

"My pastor always said
things needn't be
completely perfect
to be good."

"I didn't plan
to drive a cab,"
he said again.
Smiling.

Judy Brown, August, 22, 2010

One can hear Leon's story as just another dire indicator of an economy gone south. Or one can hear in it a generosity of spirit and kindness towards strangers, a powerful resilience, and a ministry of sharing a particular world view, a way of being in the world. Contagious. His words stay with me. "Things needn't be completely perfect to be good."

Ministry

Watching for news of that new world and nurturing the small signs

Recently I went to a big, gala event honoring a prominent leader for a lifetime of service, and as I was waiting to congratulate the honoree, I found myself in a chance conversation with a stranger also in line. I mentioned that I had just learned, to my surprise, that a mentor in my life was also a mentor to the person being honored. The stranger turned to me, smiling, and said, "Everything's connected. Everything is changing. So pay attention." And then with a smile, he walked away.

"Everything's connected. Everything is changing. So pay attention." That qualifies as a wake-up call, I thought to myself. Particularly for leaders.

Attention ☺☺ *others watch us*

Attention is everything and it is the ultimate currency of leadership. What we attend to grows. Our attention amplifies what we place it on. And, when we are leaders, others watch where we place our attention, so we need to be particularly aware of the power of our attention to amplify.

The implications of that are important. We must nurture the small signs of the things we most hope to see, the connections that support the world that we want to help create. The tiny unexpected change that is a sign of hope. The colleague who does something small or large, but remarkable, and, in its own way and time, miraculous.

Even when those sprouts of possibility appear in small, limited ways, seemingly overshadowed by the mass of woes that plague us, it is useful to remember that attention amplifies what it focuses on. Focus on what you want.

Recently, I was talking to a friend of many years, now 92, a former Nebraska football star and member of the college football hall of fame. Early in his work life, he ran a plant for Corning. I remember his telling me years ago of his frustration at the low productivity of that plant and his sense that the problem was with morale and lack of appreciation. And he didn't have a clue what to do about it. He was clearly not the "touchy-feely" type, not back then, at least. So he called in a couple of his guys, and in his then brusque way said, "I think the problem around here is not enough appreciation, so do something about it!" The guys looked puzzled, and asked how much budget they had for appreciation. "Just don't go over five bucks an appreciation," Forrey barked and sent them on their way.

About a month later, one of his engineers came in with a rose in his hand. "What in the world are you carrying a rose for, George?" Forrey asked. "The guys in finance gave it to me," said George. "What in the world are the guys in finance doing handing out roses?" barked Forrey. "Well I did something to help them out," said the engineer. Bit by bit the story emerged:

Baffled about what they could do to increase appreciation with only five dollars to work with, they were having coffee in town with a group of folks, including the man who ran the local florist shop. "Five dollars?" he asked. "For five dollars I could provide you a rose and a little paper certificate thanking the person for what he's done." It sounded like a good idea to the team.

And thus started the "rose and thank you" process. If somebody helped out a colleague, a note was written thanking the person, and the note was sent to the florist, who wrapped it around a rose, and delivered it to the person being appreciated. And, a second copy of the thank you note was taped up on the plant wall. Within six months, the 200 foot long plant wall was papered with appreciation notes as high as a man could reach, and productivity in the plant had skyrocketed, with nothing else having changed.

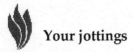 **Your jottings**

Anxiety is a prayer for what we don't want

There is a corollary to the importance of placing our attention on the early signs of what we want, and that is that if we put our attention on our anxieties, our fears, we also grow those. My friend Mary Parish reminds me, "Anxiety is the process of praying for what we don't want."

I have struggled with my own tendency to be in a constant state of high alert, of inner anxiety about what might happen, of what dire event might befall us, for which I need be fully prepared. Always having "Plan B" and "Plan C" in mind, just in case. That struggle is reflected in a poem.

The Art and Spirit of Leadership
judybrown@aol.com   www.judysorumbrown.com

The turning point

She had spent
most of life
anxious and agonizing—
unnecessarily,
as it turned out.
She even sensed
it at the time—
the senseless
waste of all
that energy.
So she decided
she would stop.
And did.
That was
the turning point.

Judy Brown June 25, 2005
From the original poem "Agonizing"

Attention is a prayer

It is easy to forget that as leaders we are often in the spotlight, and people watch us. So we need to be especially careful about where we place our focus, where and how we invest our attention. We need to remember that our attention has particular power regardless of our intent. In that sense, our attention functions as a powerful prayer—so we must place it on what we want, even when what we want seems sadly in short supply.

The technical and scientific leadership term for this approach to leadership and change is "Appreciative Inquiry," and is the work of David Cooperrider and his colleagues at Case Western Reserve. It is the step by step process of growing more of what you want by nurturing it with attention: noticing, appreciating, praising, supporting. This process, in a sense a technique, is a practice. It is a practice that requires and creates a focus on love, on passion, on what is most important to us, on what we hope for.

And an appreciative orientation is equally important when we are struggling with problems, so the intensity of our anxious attention to the mess in front of us doesn't amplify the very problem we seek to solve. The challenge is to focus on the dream, the thing we long for, what we DO want; that's what we want our attention to amplify. Yes, we have to fix things that are broken. And we must speak the honest truth about the current reality. But, our practice needs to be to focus on the dream and on the small "sprouts" of that living dream.

Being present to despair and hopelessness

Yet even when we live the practice of appreciative awareness, we often bear witness to despair, to hopelessness. Sometimes it is our own despair. Sometimes it is the despair of others.

It is challenging to be present to the darkness and the clouds (I think of Eeyore in A. A. Milne's children's stories of Winnie the Pooh) that appear to float in our collective sky.

Compassion requires that we bear witness to the despair of those around us. Yet I think bearing witness does not necessarily mean we need to give up the practice of seeing bits of the new, more hopeful world around us:

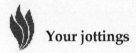 **Your jottings**

Shards

They were speaking
of their hopelessness
when he,
sitting behind me,
dropped the glass of water
and it shattered.
It was an
accident.
The conversation about
what to do if all was hopeless
carried on,
while she and I, and he,
picked up the shards of glass,
in silence,
carefully,
aware that others
would come that way barefoot
on their way to meditation
in the morning.
It took some time
to make sure
we had found
each tiny bit of broken glass.

The Art and Spirit of Leadership
judybrown@aol.com   www.judysorumbrown.com

They were still asking
what to do
when there's no hope,
when we picked up
the final shard.

Judy Brown, June 24, 2008

The Art and Spirit of Leadership
judybrown@aol.com   www.judysorumbrown.com

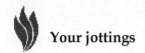 **Your jottings**

How do we, in the presence of so much challenge, despair and difficulty, practice seeking out the tiny, freshly growing sprouts of the world we long for? How do we do this and still stay connected to the tough day-to-day realities? It requires a discerning and aware eye. For me, the Montreal-born *Cirque du Soleil* has stood as a tangible example of that sort of "sprout" of a new world—one more beautiful, and more kindly, than the old circus world:

Cirque du Soleil

When I grew up
the circus
had the animals
in cages,
the elephants
in lines.

Then even as that scene
began to trouble me,
emerged within our lives
a circus of a different kind:
No animals at all,
but humans with trapezes,
trampolines and bicycles.
Instead of ropes and whips,
there were long flowing sheets
of ruby-colored silk
from which the
acrobats could swing.

What saved the animals?

Was it our seeing
what we'd done to them
and feeling bad?

judybrown@aol.com   www.judysorumbrown.com

Or was it
that the beauty
of a way
of doing "circus"
so entirely new,
swept us away,
and saved us from ourselves,
and saved the elephants
and tigers too?

Judy Brown September 26, 2000

With appreciation to

the Montreal-based *Cirque du Soleil*;
Bill McDonough, green architect;
Herman Daly, ecological economist;
Karl-Henrik Robert of Sweden's Natural Step;
Betsy Taylor of the Center for a New American Dream; and legions of leaders
everywhere
who are helping us daily
by pointing us in the direction of a way of life
more satisfying and beautiful
than the destructive practices
to which we have stubbornly and fearfully clung.

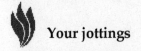 **Your jottings**

The Art and Spirit of Leadership
judybrown@aol.com   www.judysorumbrown.com

In our anxious, problem-oriented society, the idea of noticing what we want seems irresponsible. But focusing on the world we want is often the greatest of stewardship because it frees within us the energies to move forward in more constructive and healthy ways. It's interesting to note that older cultures and stories from other times can help us see the power of such an approach.

One of the best known stories about this approach, this spirit of leading and learning, comes to us from the Native American culture. It is a story of two wolves. A Cherokee grandfather is talking with his grandson and explains to the little boy that inside each of us are two wolves, always at odds with one another, always fighting. One is the wolf of anger and greed, unhappiness and struggle. And the other is the wolf of generosity and love, happiness, and peace. "But Grandfather, which one wins?" asks the grandson. "The one you feed, my son. The one you feed."

Which do we feed with our attention? Which "wolf" has center stage in our lives?

Daily practice that creates a new world

For me the most powerful story about daily attending to the work of building a new world is *The Man who Planted Trees* by the Frenchman Jean Giono. Written after World War II in response to a competition for the most hopeful story, *The Man Who Planted Trees* is the tale of a European shepherd tending his sheep on a barren landscape in the years between the world wars. His day job? To take care of his sheep. His additional practice, not on his job description as shepherd: Daily to collect acorns and at night, as the sheep are bedded down, to sit by the fire and sort out the 100 best acorns; and the next day, while walking his sheep, to poke holes with his shepherd's crook in the dirt to plant the 100 acorns from the day before.

After decades of such work, planting 100 acorns, day in and day out, the shepherd had reforested a vast landscape, which then brought other life in additional, unexpected ways: The young trees held the soil which supported other natural growth. The streams filled with water again, birds and animals returned, and the beauty of the landscape attracted the energies of young people seeking a place to build their modest homes.

In a way, the shepherd's most powerful work was invisible to the eyes of others. In Einstein's language it was "impenetrable to us (and yet it) really exists."

In fact, in Giono's story, the French forest service refers to the transformation of the landscape as a miracle, as the "spontaneous regeneration of a forest"—not unlike Sullenberger's "miracle landing" on the Hudson or the Woodcarver's bell stand, which seemed to be the "work of the spirits."

It is hard to realize or even notice that the miracle is the work of single man with his daily practice of planting acorns, while he does his "day job." It seems incomprehensible that one single man created the conditions for the transformation. His materials: time, discipline, dedication and the supportive processes of nature.

The questions posed by this story stay with me: What do I see as the lifetime of practices that help plant the seeds of the world I hope for? What are the practices that become part of the very way we do the work we've been assigned—the equivalent of our walking with the sheep and planting the acorns—that "reforest" our corner of the world?

I recall a Zen saying that seems apt here: "How you do anything is how you do everything."

Noting dream imagery

Sometimes our images of the world we dream of and want take shape in the form of actual dreams—images that emerge in the hours of sleep. Sometimes they are disturbing, sometimes inspiring. But if we are able to notice the images, without aversion, and remain curious about them—as we would react to the pattern of images in a good short story, or novel, or poem—then we might find insight in them.

In a recent course on dialogue, a woman asked me about my practice of writing in a journal each morning. "Do you write down your dreams?" she asked. I said I did, but I didn't interpret them, I just watched for patterns in images over time. "Such as?" she asked.

I wasn't expecting a follow-up question, so I was caught a little off-guard. "Well," I said, "Years back I used to regularly dream that I lived in a huge house with lots of rooms that I didn't even know about. The roof was leaking, rotting, and now and again I would venture into one of those closed-off rooms and find it full of antique grand pianos, in states of disrepair, rotting and unkempt. The images always left me distressed. The unknown rooms, the uncared for pianos, the disrepair, the leaking roofs, the sodden rotting walls—all of it unsettling."

What I didn't share with the class was that I had noticed the images and kept my own counsel about the repeated pattern. Over a period of years I made the decision to end a marriage in which my creativity was a source of derision. I began to tone down the drivenness of my work and step out from under the heavy sense of responsibility that kept me always rushing. As I was able to bring more artistry into my life, through poetry and piano playing, I stopped having the piano dreams. I fell in love with someone who had played the piano even longer than I

(I started at age 5 and he at age 3). And, there were no more piano dreams.

At least no more piano dreams until last week, when I dreamed my former husband and his girlfriend came to visit. They brought their own piano, because my ex-husband was now studying piano and he was, as his girlfriend reported, "At the senior level, and our pianos (we have three) were not good enough." I burst out laughing as I recorded that dream in my journal.

When the dialogue class was over, a senior information technology architect handed me a note on his way out the door. It said, neatly printed in the careful hand of an experienced draftsman: "Dreams are <u>answers</u> to questions we have not figured out how to ask yet." His emphasis with the underline. I have tucked his note in my journal for safe-keeping.

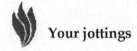 **Your jottings**

Chapter Three

Model Humor, Humanity and Humility

Where the three "H's" of this chapter came from, at first was a mystery to me. They popped into my head, as if dictated, with the lick of alliteration, like a poem often appears: "Humor, humanity, humility."

As I think about it now, it turns out they come on the heels of a youthful history in 4-H, a service program, where rural youth recite a pledge known by heart by all 4-H-ers: "I pledge my head to clearer thinking, my heart to greater loyalty, my hands to larger service, and my health to better living..." I'm tickled that after all the decades since I last had to recite that pledge I can still recall the words. So it must be that for me these three H's of humor, humanity and humility build naturally on the earlier four.

Humor: When I ask people about leaders who have brought out the very best in them, where they have felt most alive, and most engaged (my practical language for pointing toward a spirited workplace), they almost always mention the power of a playful and self-deprecating sense of humor.

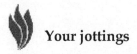 **Your jottings**

The words of leadership

The words of leadership
are words of humor too,
of laughter,
like the wind that tickles
leaves in autumn,
and lighten us as days grow long,
so humor heals and helps prepare us
for the winters of our work.

Judy Brown, November 17, 2000

The Art and Spirit of Leadership
judybrown@aol.com   www.judysorumbrown.com

A leader's lightness of spirit and sense of humor can turn around the darkest day. Consider the words of James Thurber, one of America's great humorists:

> Humor is a serious thing. I like to think of it as one of our greatest earliest natural resources, which must be preserved at all cost.

But Thurber makes it clear that all humor is not equal, and the distinctions he makes seem to me particularly important in the world of leadership:

> The wit makes fun of other persons; the satirist makes fun of the world; the humorist makes fun of himself, but in so doing, he identifies himself with people—that is, people everywhere—not for the purpose of taking them apart, but simply revealing their true nature.

I grew up in a family with a zany yet kindly sense of humor, where puns were an art form, and light-hearted laughter was part of all gatherings. We often read Thurber out loud. As I think about it now, it was probably Thurber's unconscious influence that inspired my brother David in many of his zany adventures, the most famous of which is the "car in the lake" episode: David and his pals had driven the family car out on the ice on the 22 mile-long lake in front of our house. This was not unusual, as we learned to be skilled winter drivers by driving on the frozen lake.

But that night, he neglected to avoid the spot where a spring had thinned the ice. And he dropped the car into 20 feet of water. He and his pals escaped unharmed, but the car remained on the bottom. So David called his wife to report he'd be a little late. "I am having car trouble," he reported calmly. "What's the problem," she asked. "I think it's flooded," he responded. (Flooded being a term for a car refusing to start because there was too much gas on the sparkplugs.)

75

The Art and Spirit of Leadership
judybrown@aol.com   www.judysorumbrown.com

So, humor played a big role in my early life. Even my dissertation reflected it—a study of the world view of comedy in Shakespeare and Moliere's works. As has my life-time fascination with surprise and humanity's odd quirks.

While we read a lot of Thurber when I was growing up, in the serious intervening years of my life, I'd somehow lost sight of the particular brand of Thurber humor. And as friends will remind me, I even lost the ready sense of humor that had once been my hallmark. My practice in subsequent years has been to reclaim that sense of humor by noticing more quickly the way in which the universe is ever ready with its own quirky sense of humor, its playful examples of the absurdly and beautifully human.

Recently Thurber reappeared in my life in one of those "out of the blue" surprises: One of my graduate students began the preface to his final paper in my leadership course, with Thurber's famous story "The Unicorn in the Garden," without comment. I am still curious about the many messages it offers—for the student who included it, and for me. Thurber wrote:

> Once upon a sunny morning a man who sat in a breakfast nook looked up from his scrambled eggs to see a white unicorn with a golden horn quietly cropping the roses in the garden. The man went up to the bedroom where his wife was still asleep and woke her. "There's a unicorn in the garden," he said. "Eating roses." She opened one unfriendly eye and looked at him.
>
> "The unicorn is a mythical beast," she said, and turned her back on him. The man walked slowly downstairs and out into the garden. The unicorn was still there; now he was browsing among the tulips. "Here, unicorn," said the man, and he pulled up a lily and gave it to him. The unicorn ate it gravely. With a high heart, because there was a unicorn in his garden, the man went upstairs and roused his wife

The Art and Spirit of Leadership
judybrown@aol.com   www.judysorumbrown.com

again. "The unicorn," he said, "ate a lily." His wife sat up in bed and looked at him coldly.

"You are a booby," she said, "and I am going to have you put in the booby-hatch."

The man, who had never liked the words "booby" and "booby-hatch," and who liked them even less on a shining morning when there was a unicorn in the garden, thought for a moment. "We'll see about that," he said. He walked over to the door. "He has a golden horn in the middle of his forehead," he told her. Then he went back to the garden to watch the unicorn; but the unicorn had gone away. The man sat down among the roses and went to sleep.

As soon as the husband had gone out of the house, the wife got up and dressed as fast as she could. She was very excited and there was a gloat in her eye. She telephoned the police and she telephoned a psychiatrist; she told them to hurry to her house and bring a strait-jacket. When the police and the psychiatrist arrived they sat down in chairs and looked at her, with great interest.

"My husband," she said, "saw a unicorn this morning." The police looked at the psychiatrist and the psychiatrist looked at the police. "He told me it ate a lily," she said. The psychiatrist looked at the police and the police looked at the psychiatrist. "He told me it had a golden horn in the middle of its forehead," she said. At a solemn signal from the psychiatrist, the police leaped from their chairs and seized the wife. They had a hard time subduing her, for she put up a terrific struggle, but they finally subdued her. Just as they got her into the strait-jacket, the husband came back into the house.

The Art and Spirit of Leadership
judybrown@aol.com   www.judysorumbrown.com

"Did you tell your wife you saw a unicorn?" asked the police. "Of course not," said the husband. "The unicorn is a mythical beast." "That's all I wanted to know," said the psychiatrist. "Take her away. I'm sorry, sir, but your wife is as crazy as a jaybird."

So they took her away, cursing and screaming, and shut her up in an institution. The husband lived happily ever after.

I think what touches me in this story is not just the humor of it, but the sense that as a friend said, "Sometimes the good guys win."

Sometimes the person who sees what others don't see, who sees possibilities, who dreams, who is imaginative, can make a huge impact and nurture a more beautiful life. Contribute to what matters most. Get important work out the door. Save our lives.

And then sometimes, no one seems to see the unicorn in the garden at all, or whoever sees it is cowed into silence by others who don't see the mythical beast.

Skillfully debated into silence.

One need only return to the report from the 9/11 Commission to recall that what brought down the twin towers of the World Trade Center was not a failure of intelligence but rather a failure of imagination: the inability to imagine something beyond our experience, to imagine why someone could be interested in the capacity to fly a commercial airliner, but not interested in learning how to land one.

That is perhaps our modern-day equivalent of the unicorn in the garden. Eating the roses.

Humanity: In a sense, Thurber's notion about the humorist, as distinguished from the wit and the satirist, leads us to the importance of the leader being at one with all of humanity, of being able to poke fun at herself, to see the humor in her own situation. And in so doing make it possible for others to appreciate that we are all human, all equal, all connected, all vulnerable in our own way, all on one kind of journey or another.

Being at one with humanity and our vulnerabilities

The practice of being at one with humanity shows up in many ways. My most powerful experience with it came decades back, when I was facing daunting interviews as a candidate for the White House Fellows Program. A phone call came from a stranger. The man explained that he worked at the Pentagon and he had seen the list indicating that I was among the last 32 candidates for 15 slots as a White House Fellow.

Then he explained his reason for calling: "A few years back," he said, "the Army nominated me for the Fellowship program. I knew nothing about the program. And I had no idea what to expect. Going into the interview process without knowing anyone who had been through it, without knowing what to expect, was really unnerving to me—unsettling. So my reason for calling is to give you my name and phone number, so if it would be helpful for you to talk about the process, or even practice some questions with me, I'm here and I'd be happy to help. I realize your experience will be different from mine, but still, I just wouldn't want you to have to go through this without someone to call on, if that would be helpful. I don't want you to have to go through what I went through alone."

I was a little startled by the frankness of this stranger about what he'd been through and also his willingness to help me. I carefully took down his phone number. It was a 703 area code—the Pentagon. And his name: Colin Powell.

Not a famous name back then. Now a household word—the man who went on to be head of the US Joint Chiefs of Staff and US Secretary of State. I didn't call him back before my interview. It seemed unnecessary and besides his call had already helped me to feel less anxious.

What has stayed with me from this experience is the way Colin Powell approached our conversation: He could have told me he succeeded in the interview process and was selected. He didn't say that. He could have told me he knew all the answers. He didn't say that either.

He simply told me that he suffered from feeling alone and not knowing what to expect and he didn't want me to have to go through that.

As the years passed, Colin Powell and I were part of the alumni network of the White House Fellows Program. I watched the upward arc of his career and appreciated the many ways he continued to contribute to leadership in the public domain. But it seemed that for all his evident discipline and hard work, it was his humanity, vulnerability and generosity of spirit in that long-ago phone call that explained his rise to prominence to me.

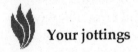 **Your jottings**

To speak from the heart

To speak from the heart,
is a practice
of living—
not to be measured
in the scale of
"Did it work? Did
what I say change
how the other thought?
Get me the answer
I was yearning for?"
Not to be measured
in the cup of
"Was it quite enough,
too little, or too much?"
Or by econometrics of
"Did it return me
what I wanted?"
To speak from center
of the heart
is to exercise
our humanity,
as if it were
a muscle
to be strengthened
for the
long, long journey
of a life.

Judy Brown, March 16, 2004

The Art and Spirit of Leadership
judybrown@aol.com   www.judysorumbrown.com

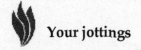 **Your jottings**

Humanity's darker side

While I am reminded that human beings have a light and generous side, they also have a darker strain that we must acknowledge as well, not only around us but within us. Those who study dreams, and who call that darker side the "shadow side," are particularly sensitive to the darker dynamics of being human.

It's not easy, not pleasurable, to look at the parts of being human that are less positive. It takes a calm honesty. Perhaps for all of us it is natural to think of ourselves as part of the "good guys" and some other group – the violent, the political extremists, however we characterize the "other" —as the "bad guys."

Dealing with our dark side demands a deeper, open-eyed awareness that we are far from perfect. It is part of the practice of being human (and the practice of wise leadership) to know that both the good and the bad are resident within each of us. It is our practice and our attention that invite out one or the other. As the Cherokee grandfather would remind us, each moment we are choosing which "wolf" to feed, which "wolf" we pay attention to. But like the Cherokee grandfather, we are well served to remain always aware of both "wolves."

And so some of life's surprises are about the darker side, closer to home than we realize, that we need to look full in the face. That notion turns me to a strange story from my own family that keeps that awareness always in my own mind. It is another story of a stranger, this time a violent one.

All families have, I suspect, their own brand of secrets, things that one knows just not to talk about. In our family, the secret was about my mother. Her Swiss immigrant mother, my grandmother, had died young leaving 7 children, the youngest 6 months old, the eldest 17. Mother at 11 was in the middle.

The Art and Spirit of Leadership
judybrown@aol.com   www.judysorumbrown.com

Her father, my grandfather, abandoned the children and was never seen again. It was understood that he had died. But there were many parts of the story that were left untold. What had happened? What was he really like? Who was this grandfather whose name could not be mentioned?

We only knew that Mother was on her own at 11, the hinted history being that she was a house servant to several families until she was "adopted" by a family who needed help with their children. There she stayed through high school and beyond, until she went to work as a book-keeper and met and married my father. They had two children, first me and then my brother David.

Both David and I knew never to ask Mother about her biological family, particularly her father. It provoked an icy silence, dark moods and never yielded any information. So early on we stopped asking. Dad didn't seem to know anything either—I expected he'd learned not to ask as well.

Years passed. Mother had died of heart disease just like her mother. David and his family had come to live on a farm not far from where we'd lived and about 20 miles from where Mother had grown up. I was living in the Washington, DC area by then. One day David called and said, "We have an aunt in Texas." Oddly, I was in Texas leading a retreat at that moment, and I was more startled than curious. I was sure we didn't have an aunt in Texas. So I asked him why he thought so, and he replied "It's a long story. I'll tell you sometime."

Over time, this is the story that emerged: Just down the dirt road from where David and his wife lived, another family moved in. Not local. From away. Strangers. But one day, David's wife told him that she had heard that the husband had turned violent toward the wife (how she knew, I don't know—but in small rural areas, stories get around) and she thought perhaps David should

84   The Art and Spirit of Leadership
             judybrown@aol.com   www.judysorumbrown.com

go down there and try to talk some sense into the husband, who was about David's age.

So David trudged down the dirt road and knocked on the neighbor's door. When the door opened, the husband, the stranger, was standing with a shot-gun aimed at David's chest. We came from a hunting family, so the shot-gun was not a shock, but the target was. David backed away, and went home. Probably feeling less than courageous, but in my eyes, having been pretty smart.

That incident with the man with the shot-gun, naturally made David curious about who the stranger was and where he'd come from. And one day, talking with the old cherry farmer across the road, David found out. The old neighbor said that the violent stranger was a relative of occasional guests from Texas who stayed with the cherry farmer. By teasing out the details, David learned that the man with the shot-gun was the grandson of a man who had once lived in Traverse City where Mother had grown up, a man who had moved down to Texas decades back where he raised a family. His name, the grand-father of the shot-gun toting stranger, was Perry Burgess. The only thing we knew about our long-believed-dead grandfather was his name: Perry Burgess.

In a moment David pieced together the puzzle. Our grandfather had not died after all. He had abandoned his Michigan family, gone to Texas (which was why we had an aunt there) and started a new family. One grandson of that family had moved north, and Heaven only knows how such things happen, chosen to live on a dirt road in the next house down from another grandson, my brother David, neither of them with any clue of the link between them.

The violent man who had nearly shot my brother, was our cousin.

Having a sense of our humanity means acknowledging that the violent, dark DNA is a shared one—in our case literally shared. Brother David and I and the violent stranger have the same grandfather.

But in human terms, it is always so; the violence is a part of each of us, part of our family tree. It is knowing the truth of that which opens us to the practice of accepting people, including ourselves, with their full humanity, with their faults, even with their evil acts, because in a deep sense we know we come from the same stock. Accepting. And yet always seeking our higher angels. And being mindful that the inner terrain, our inner council, the inner voice, represent both the higher angels and the bare human instincts that we see all around us in the world.

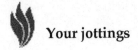 **Your jottings**

No magic answers

No magic answers.
Life is a miracle,
a blessing.
And when all is tangled,
twisted, in a knot,
there is no magic answer,
only appreciation for the humanness,
the grief, compassion;
only those faithful things
will save us.
It is a risky business, life is—
and there is
no magic answer.

Judy Brown, January 23, 2008

The Art and Spirit of Leadership
judybrown@aol.com   www.judysorumbrown.com

All of these things

All of these things
that all of us
now represent—
the quietness,
quick humor,
pensiveness,
penchant for action,
gift for questions,
opinion on the quick,
the sudden judgment
wondering
and loving,
fear—
All those
quite human sides
that we have seen
in one another,
here and there,
are also represented
in the inner circle
of our soul.

When we are able
to give space
to all within,
admitting them
to light,
we then give space
to all around us
just as easily,
without an effort,
without strain,
knowing that each
is a part of all.

Judy Brown, March 18, 2004

The Art and Spirit of Leadership
judybrown@aol.com   www.judysorumbrown.com

Humility: I was tickled to find out that in his autobiography Benjamin Franklin listed twelve virtues that he was working on, with the help of a checklist and an exacting spread-sheet, long before the advent of Excel. He was convinced these were the key to being a better person. (I'm reminded of a CEO friend whose response to my question, "How are you?" often is, "Trying daily to be a better person," a modern-day Benjamin Franklin.)

A friend of Franklin's, perhaps noting the tinge of arrogance in the very idea that one could become perfect through the pursuit of twelve virtues, suggested to him that he add a thirteenth: humility. Ever paying attention to feedback, Franklin added it. Perhaps we would all do well to add humility to our list: our "to do" list of practices, and our "to be" list of qualities.

We may think of humility as a matter of modesty, and not placing ourselves in some kind of exalted rank, living with a "bowed head." In a sense, humility offers us perspective, the ability to not take ourselves, our efforts and our roles so seriously. It keeps us free of grandiosity. So we might see humility, like humor, as being a quality of "lightening up." Or as one participant in a retreat responded when I asked her to translate the Greek words on her sweatshirt: "'All things in moderation', otherwise known as," she added with a quick smile, "'No freaking out.'" No freaking out. Equanimity. Perspective. A longer view of things, and a much longer view of our place in things.

In *The Book of Awakening* Mark Nepo says of humility, "Humility, which comes from the word *humus*, the soil, offers more than a bowed head. It gives us a connection with everything older than we are and so provides us with a calming perspective outside of our daily worries, and often beyond our understanding." There are moments in our life that place us naturally in that place of humility. Perhaps such moments are the natural path to Franklin's thirteenth virtue.

The Art and Spirit of Leadership
judybrown@aol.com   www.judysorumbrown.com

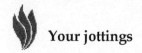 **Your jottings**

For me, such a sense of humility is almost always shaped by the power and perspective of the natural world. By the long view and a sense of how small we are against that natural backdrop. As I was writing this, the experience of humility that came most fully to mind was a March day years back, when I walked the Lake Michigan beach in Northern Michigan.

Ten thousand years ago

Ten thousand years ago
this beach was like it is today.
Before the Europeans,
maybe even before tribes,
there were these sand expanses
and the ragged bluffs,
the breathing of the waves,
the islands, Manitou and Fox,
the distant promontories
that have Western names now —
Whaleback and Pyramid Point.
All stood like this,
the vast expanse,
completely,
absolutely desolate
and beautiful.

Today, bundled against
the winter wind,
I walk alone toward
the north. I walk a
steady pace an hour,
then turning back, I
walk another hour.

In all that time,
in all that space,
I see no other human face,
nor any footprint,
nor any sign of human habitation,
only the waves,
the light, the sand,
the rocks,
only the solitude
of God,
only the Spirit
of this place.

Judy Brown, March 28, 2002

The Art and Spirit of Leadership
judybrown@aol.com www.judysorumbrown.com

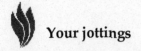 **Your jottings**

Chapter Four

Practice Generous, Wide Curiosity

Eleanor Roosevelt once said, "I think, at a child's birth, if a mother could ask a fairy godmother to endow it with the most useful gift, that gift should be curiosity."

Wisdom begins in wonder.

After the first year of a new leadership development program in the field of services and support for elders, one of the young leaders who had been part of the program sent me a brass bookmark that I carry with me everywhere. Inscribed on it are words from Socrates: "Wisdom begins in wonder."

I love the pun I find in Socrates' words: Is it "wonder" as in "I wonder how that works?" "I wonder what surprise is around the corner?"

Or is it "wonder" as in "a sense of wonder," a sense of "awe," seeing the world as wonderful, awesome: "It's a wonder to me...." Allowing ourselves to be delighted in what we find. As our young folks say these days, "Awesome."

Whichever side of the pun we choose, wonder and curiosity seem to me to be on the path to wisdom. It is the wonder and curiosity often seen in children, in great scientists, and in artists. It is a certain presence and quality of attention.

The Art and Spirit of Leadership
judybrown@aol.com   www.judysorumbrown.com

The artist pays attention

The artist
pays attention,
notices,
takes in —
the light,
the earth,
the shimmer
and the solid dirt —
how many colors —
grey and pewter,
silver, platinum,
shiny and dull,
make up the ice
upon a frozen
tidal creek
in January.

The palette
is much richer
than it seems
at first.

More colors,
tones,
and textures
than the eye
that knows
this territory
sees.
And overlooks.

It is the eye
that doesn't know,
that spends time
being curious,
aware,
taking in
the all of it—
that comes
to see it all.

Judy Brown, January 5, 2011

The Art and Spirit of Leadership
judybrown@aol.com www.judysorumbrown.com

The space of wondering, of wide curiosity, of not knowing, seems indeed to be the space in which wisdom can grow. Yet it demands a change in how we approach things, a change in practice. It requires that we loosen our grip on our certainties; that for a few minutes we give up our assumptions; that we develop, almost as second nature, the habit of wondering about all kinds of important (and seemingly unimportant) things; that we cultivate the practice of wondering about even the smallest and seemingly most inconsequential of things: "I wonder what that little ripple is in the stream. What lives down there?" "I wonder where the word 'threshold' came from?" I wonder.

Why would we want to practice wondering about the seemingly inconsequential? Because we really don't know what is inconsequential. Our ideas of what is worthy of our noticing are habitual and may limit what we are able to see, at all. So, one important practice is to stretch our curiosity towards a wider and wider ranging perception, a sweeping sense of wonder.

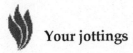 **Your jottings**

Each day dawns

Each day dawns
with its own
discoveries and surprise,
with its gifts.
If we are home
to all of that
we can't be lost.

Judy Brown, August 17, 2005

The Art and Spirit of Leadership
judybrown@aol.com   www.judysorumbrown.com

The ancient Socratic quotation, "Wisdom begins in wonder," suggests that the notion of the value of curiosity is far from new. It is a theme that emerges throughout the ages and across cultures. In his book about Leonardo daVinci, *Learning to Think Like Leonardo*, Michael Gelb lists *"curiosita"* as the first of the seven qualities that Leonardo embodied and that we would do well to emulate. Yet as leaders we are pushed to be certain, to come to a conclusion, to decide. Quickly. To stop wondering and get on with it.

Research on human perception reminds us that as soon as we decide, we have narrowed the range of data of which we are conscious. After all, our mind has a lot of work to do, and it needs to be as efficient as possible, so it only pays attention to information that is either confirming or contradicting our theory of what's going on.

Thus, before the twin towers came down on September 11, 2001, it was hard for the intelligence community as a whole to "see" the information about people learning to fly big aircraft, but not caring much about landing them. They had no theory that would help them understand or consider such behavior. The events of September 11, 2001, explained why. Until then, the data were pointless, because they did not fit any theory we were testing.

But, it is not easy to shift from our certainties, our judgments, our current understanding, to an open curiosity. It feels odd. It feels as though we are wasting time. As if we are being less than "focused," less than efficient. All shifts in attention feel odd at first, because we have habits of attention. We are comfortable with our usual way of acting, our habitual way of thinking.

It takes intention and practice to make the shift from the old to the new, but practicing the new makes a difference in what we can see. With intentionally more curious behavior, as in all changes we seek to make, practice increases our skill and capacity—and eventually we find ourselves more habitually curious. At first, the practices may seem bulky or cumbersome, but over time they begin to be second nature. Open, generous curiosity becomes a more natural state. Almost automatic. And some day down the line, we realize that curiosity has become an inherent part of our nature.

Becoming naturally curious

How do we create a "practice" of curiosity in a world which pushes us towards knowing, towards judgment, towards closure, towards certainty? For me there are five fundamental practices that I use to loosen the hold that my desire for certainty has on me. The five are:

> 1) *The Rule of Six*
> 2) *Cone in the Box*
> 3) *The Ladder of Inference*
> 4) *The Outrage Loop*
> 5) *Softball Questions.*

These practices move us toward a natural, authentic curiosity about ourselves, about others, and about the world around us. They are practices that can keep us in closer touch with reality. And reality is always our friend—not an easy friendship certainly—yet a friend without whom we cannot make a helpful, healthy difference in this world.

The Rule of Six

The Rule of Six is a Native American practice for expanding the possible theories we might hold about an event, or something that is challenging us. It requires that we come up with six possible theories of what's going on, and as we do, we expand the data we are conscious of. Six ways to think about what we might call a problem. Thus we are less likely to move forward precipitously and dangerously.

How do we use *The Rule of Six* ? I say to groups I am working with, "Think of something that you are trying to figure out, that is important, and that baffles you. For instance, an employee who is underperforming."

"So what's our first theory about what's going on? Mine is usually that the person is lazy, not nearly as hard working as I thought, unmotivated."

People nod. But then someone says, "Maybe the person doesn't know how to do the job."

"Or," someone else chimes in, "Maybe they have trouble at home."

Another says, "Or they have responsibility for an aging parent."

Someone else adds, "Maybe they are sick and just got a scary diagnosis."

"Or," says another, "They are sick but they don't realize it yet."

Within minutes, the group has spun out six credible theories for why the person might be underperforming. I admit to the group that if I'd latched onto the first idea that sprang into my mind (lazy, unmotivated), I'd have opted for either firing them or trying to inspire them. Neither of which would provide much leverage on a health problem.

Generating the six possibilities makes us curious about what might be going on—even beyond the six. "Yes, but," people squawk, "We have to make quick decisions. We can't be spinning out six possibilities when we have to make a decision."

The Art and Spirit of Leadership
judybrown@aol.com www.judysorumbrown.com

"Oh," I explain, "*The Rule of Six* doesn't suggest not acting. You must move forward in responsible ways. *The Rule of Six* only requires holding six possibilities in your consciousness and continuing to learn from incoming data about all six possibilities. It doesn't stop you from acting; it only increases the likelihood that you will notice more data and act more responsibly and wisely."

"With *The Rule of Six*, your decision is a working hypothesis, not an unchangeable decision. For instance, after consideration, you might not opt for the 'quick fix' resulting from your favorite or first conclusion. You might instead, having in mind several possibilities, choose to have a conversation with the employee about what you are observing, and an open inquiry about what, from the employee's point of view, is going on. "

"Well," folks will say, "The employee example is an easy one, but can this be used on big organizational matters? On more complex matters?"

"Yes," I say, taking a deep breath. "I used it once on a family business dilemma that had the potential to bankrupt our family." Reluctant to revisit the painful events that prompted this use of *The Rule of Six*, nonetheless, I fess up:

> Many years back our family had a large Holstein dairy operation on the high plateau of Western Maryland. In partnership with a local family (we lived near Washington DC and had jobs there), we milked 70 some cows, and had close to 150 animals. And each year, for about 10 years, it seemed as if the dairy farm was just about to break even. But it never did. It was beautiful, but a continual economic drain.

The Art and Spirit of Leadership
judybrown@aol.com   www.judysorumbrown.com

Each year one crisis or another hit us. One year the snows closed the road to the farm, and we had to dump milk on the snow because the milk truck couldn't get to us. Another year, there was an invisible problem with stray voltage, so when each cow tried to drink water from her drinking fountain in the milking barn, she got a shock on her nose, so she stopped drinking and the milk production went down. It took months to figure out the problem and fix it.

And everything was heavily mortgaged—even the cows— so the operation had huge downside potential for everyone associated with it. It needed every penny of income it could produce.

I had grown so desperately frustrated with the financial pressures of this enterprise, and the sense of personal responsibility to earn more and more money to keep it afloat, that I was ready to pitch the whole thing—close it down. Even if it bankrupted us.

But thankfully, on a drive from Maine to Maryland to handle yet another crisis, we began to explore *The Rule of Six*, to sketch scenarios for the future of the farm.

One was the dairy farm equivalent of a "nuclear winter" scenario: we sell everything, land, cows, farm machinery, everything, and figure on bankruptcy.

But as we talked, other possibilities emerged as well. We could sell just the cows, and get out of the dairy business entirely, then we could rent the dairy barn and milking operation to someone else who had cows. So that was option two. Seemed unlikely, but not impossible.

Or we could turn the 450 acres back into a crop farm and lease it back to the Mennonite family from whom we'd bought it. No cows on the land at all. It was not clear how that would work economically, but it was credible. It became option three.

Option number four was to link up the farm with a nearby university environmental education program and have the farm function as an environmental learning lab. That fit our values as educators and environmentalists.

Option five came out of my leadership work: we could use the house and land as a retreat center for executives wanting to learn leadership in a natural setting, and to learn the leadership lessons that we can take from nature.

And option six, seemingly way out, but appealing to my animal-loving step-son, was to turn it into an animal rescue site. Well, there it was. Six possible paths.

"So what happened?" people asked me eagerly.

"In an odd way, almost every scenario came into play over the twenty years that followed that conversation." I said. "We did sell the cows and managed to lease the dairy operation to another family that owned cows but had just lost their lease." That took some pressure off us. After that it be came clear that we had other options than to be dairy farmers ourselves.

Then one day a rat chewed through a wire in the dairy barn, and the place caught fire. The barn burned to the ground. Thank Heavens the people's cows were all out in the pastures! A knee-jerk reaction might have been to rebuild immediately, but because we had so many possible scenarios conscious in our minds, we took a breath and decided not to rebuild, using the insurance settlement to pay off our debt. That, too, gave us some breathing room.

Then, no longer needing the land to support a sizable dairy herd, we invited the Mennonite family who had had been the prior owners of most of the acreage, to lease it back as a crop farm. They were happy to do that, and to this day they maintain the crop farming operation. And without dairy partners who needed housing, we could rent out the houses. That provided some new income.

I experimented with retreats and leadership programs at the farm, but soon learned that catering for large groups, out of a one hundred year old barn was far from my true calling. Those who came thoroughly enjoyed the experience, particularly one of the sessions led by Native American educator Paula Underwood, who had first taught me *The Rule of Six*. Paula and I organized a program on what Native Americans could teach corporate America about leading change. I can still see the group of us in the old barn, sitting in a big circle on hay bales, while Paula sketched *The Rule of Six* on the newsprint tacked to the grain bin and the children played up in the hay mows.

The possibility of an environmental center linked to the area university didn't seem to reap any short-term benefits, although it still could result in a partnership.

My animal-loving stepson has since turned one of the barns into a pig rescue center. It began years back when flooding in the mid-west sent pigs onto the levees, where people were shooting them. He rescued a mother pig, who is now, I understand, enormous and is living a luxurious (in pig terms) life with her offspring in western Maryland.

The Art and Spirit of Leadership
judybrown@aol.com   www.judysorumbrown.com

Like the complicated dairy story, most complex organizational challenges can be approached more wisely with the discipline of *The Rule of Six*. The practice of slowing down and stepping back, allows for visualizing more possibilities. Rather than settling on one of them as the absolute truth, the process of holding and exploring a variety of possibilities helps us see openings and emerging opportunities that otherwise might be invisible or that we would ignore.

Cone in the Box

Cone in the Box is a visual antidote to our natural tendency to screen out data at odds with our perceptions and point of view. It is a practice that helps us become genuinely curious, rather than resistant to that which at first glance seems wrong, or startling, or simply at odds with what we have known to be true.

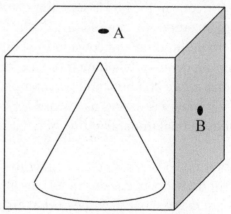

Cone in the Box was another "out of the blue" experience for me. It was my Center for Creative Leadership colleague, Bob Ginnett, who introduced the *Cone in the Box* to a group of executives sitting in quietly simmering resistance in a seminar on dialogue skills I was teaching. Realizing that these executives, sent by their bosses to have their communication skills "fixed," were not buying into the ideas on dialogue that I was offering, Bob stepped to the front of the room, sketched a cone in a box and said, "This picture explains why dialogue is a critical leadership skill and it also explains why airplanes crash."

These executives had flown into Colorado for this seminar and would have to fly out. So they were all suddenly interested, if not

The Art and Spirit of Leadership
judybrown@aol.com   www.judysorumbrown.com

in dialogue, at least in airplane crashes. And Bob's research passion was teams, particularly airplane cockpit teams.

His sketch was of a three dimensional cone resting on the floor of a closed box. The closed box had only two vantage points from which to view the cone. One was at the top looking down on the cone. Peephole A. The second was on the side of the box looking in at the side of the cone. Peephole B.

Folks at the Peephole A vantage point would report seeing a circle. Those looking in at the side from vantage point B would report seeing a triangle. None of our usual methods for resolving such a difference (debating, arguing, voting, out-ranking and power politics) is of any value here, because each vantage point is right, but it is also incomplete, insufficient, partial.

If the cone in the box is something of major importance to the organization, we can't learn what is true of it, what is really there, without holding and considering both perspectives simultaneously. Gaining more information about each perspective and how and why people at that vantage point see what they see, moves us toward a more complex, multi-dimensional understanding of what really is in front of us.

The single skill that helps us gain more information is to ask genuinely open, curious questions about how the other person has come to see what they see—what experience, what perspective shapes their perception?

Only by being curious about how the other has come to see what she sees can we create an understanding that is whole and durable.

There are two key practices that the *Cone in the Box* instills in us. The first is the ability to stay in the space of observation, rather than judgment. When I say "I see a circle," rather than "It's a

108   The Art and Spirit of Leadership

circle," I am staying in the space of observation and out of the space of conclusion. The shift from reporting what we see, to making an assessment of what it is, becomes a movement away from learning and into certain conflict. That conflict usually gets resolved in a way that stops us from learning; it gets resolved by rank, power, voting or debating.

The second key practice that *Cone in the Box* instills in us is the practice of being faithful to what we see and being honest about it, realizing that to mince our words, to give up our perspective, may put our lives at risk. It may crash the plane. At the same time we must be open to and invite opposing points of view, because we need them in order to have all the facts and thus avoid crashing the plane. We must be clear in our own perspective and open to and curious about the perspective of others. Simultaneously.

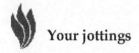 **Your jottings**

Certainty

Certainty
gives way
to curiosity,
and wonder,
sometimes,
when we're
the most
alive.
Like birds
dive into water
after fish,
we are fearless
and hungry
for the truth,
for things
out of our sight,
for life itself.

Judy Brown, December 23, 2006

The Ladder of Inference

The *Ladder of Inference* is an individual and collective analytical method for looking with open eyes at what shapes our conclusions, our judgments and our movement to action. It allows us to explore whether we still see those influences as sound and it gives us the skills to talk with our colleagues about the steps on our ladder, to inquire about ladders that have brought them to their conclusions.

Long a practice of the organizational learning community at MIT that has evolved from the initial work of Peter Senge and his colleagues, the *Ladder of Inference* helps us sort out within ourselves, and then with one another, the steps that have brought us to our conclusions. How did we come to this decision? What data? What experience? What assumptions? What values? What thinking? What emotions? Once we are able to determine with some clarity and honesty the steps in our own movement to action, we can then share that chain of events and thinking with our colleagues (even those jumps we take when the conclusions seem obvious to us). As we understand the "steps" of our own

The Art and Spirit of Leadership
judybrown@aol.com   www.judysorumbrown.com

thinking more completely, we can then invite our colleagues to let us know how they got to where they are.

This process reminds us that in any meeting of a group of people, even people sharing the same purpose and goals, each person is usually sitting on the top of her own *Ladder of Inference* –perched at the top of her own ladder of reasoning for her choices and actions. It is as though fifteen team members are on fifteen separate ladders around the table.

The insight of the *Ladder* helps us realize that making statements, drawing conclusions, advocating a particular position, moves things up the ladder, towards conclusion and action. Asking open and curious questions leads us back down to the base of the ladder, to the data, experience, perspectives of the group and can be useful for reviewing the assumptions that might be limiting and tangling us up.

It also gives us a light-hearted way to catch ourselves and to catch each other when we are "high on the ladder," that is, when we have so much experience and certainty that we have neglected to check out the data anew or to consider whether our assumptions remain valid. One can say, "I think I have been operating pretty high on the ladder here and I want to test out my assumptions with you." Or one can say, playfully, "Whoa, I think we are pretty high on the ladder here. What data are we looking at?"

And a quiet conversation sharing our thinking about a particular work issue, mapped on the ladder, can help us shift perspective. One man, after such a conversation said, "I think I'm missing a few rungs on my ladder. And what I called data turned out to be assumptions." Breakthrough!

The Outrage Loop

The Outrage Loop is an individual and collective method for looking at why our certainties are so intense. I invented it when I repeatedly caught myself being outraged well beyond what circumstances warranted. (So, take this as permission to create practices of your own that work for you and that you can share with others.) It is a practice that helps me loosen my certainties and to become curious about my inner processes and my reactions.

It allows one to step back, for a moment, from the certainty that we are right. (In my case certainties often show up as outrage.) We can take a breath, wonder why we feel so intensely about what's right in this case and inquire gently within ourselves about what assumptions we need let go in order to see the situation more clearly, fully and realistically.

> A participant asks, "Can you give us an example?"
> I respond, "The silliest one, and the one that really taught me this practice, was an experience with a lady cutting strawberries."

> "First you should know that I come from a family that raised thirty-two tons of strawberries a summer. I picked berries, sorted berries. I was an absolute expert on how to handle strawberries. Of course that was many years ago. And this is a recent story. That alone should be a clue to me that I am on shaky territory with my outrage"

> "At 7 o'clock one morning, I stopped for coffee at a little French café near work, and saw a woman across the counter slicing strawberries in half to serve as garnishes for entrees. I was appalled at how she was doing it. With a narrow 12- inch bread knife lying sharp edge up, she was sliding the big berries onto the knife, and letting the two

The Art and Spirit of Leadership
judybrown@aol.com www.judysorumbrown.com

halves fall to either side. 'Wrong!' cried out every bone in my body. Outraged. Just Wrong. And besides, not safe. My family is rabid about safety, so after wrong, not safe takes control."

"I forced myself to pay attention to my unnecessary intensity. I took a breath. I asked myself what was I assuming and how did this lady with the bread knife challenge that assumption and thus 'outrage' me? I mused about what I could learn about myself from this experience."

"Clearly I assumed there was just one way to slice strawberries, and that I had the right answer. (And likely there were other places in my life where I operated in the same way, with the same huge expenditure of energy, I said to myself.)"

"I realized that when my initial reaction is to cite safety as a reason for something being wrong, it is possible I am over-reacting and using safety as an excuse to be outraged."

"I realized that when my initial reaction is outrage, even over a small issue, it's likely I am over-reacting. Placing too much importance on my way of doing something."

The practice of noticing undue intensity and gently inquiring into its source allows us to loosen the hold of that source on us and to be more in touch with the reality of the current moment.

A way to be

To look
at provocation
through
the lens
of curiosity,
that is
the way to be
free
in this world.

Judy Brown, April 11, 2009

The Art and Spirit of Leadership
judybrown@aol.com   www.judysorumbrown.com

Softball Questions

Softball Questions is another practice that I use to help move us to a space of curiosity. This is the practice of interacting with someone only with questions, not with statements, and only with questions that reflect open curiosity. Gentle questions.

This practice of posing questions that only the other person can answer comes from the centuries old tradition of the Society of Friends in which the process extends for three full hours—a person with a dilemma receiving questions only and answering those questions, or taking them under advisement.

To think about. The person is held safe by the rule of double confidentiality: no one will ever speak of what was said in the gathering, and no one will ever approach the person and ask "follow-up" questions—"didja, didn'tja" etc.

It is a powerful process that can be very helpful in our hurry-up- and- judge world. Parker Palmer has adapted that old process from the faith tradition and introduced it into the courage and renewal work.

The ultimate test of the quality of a softball question is this: Is this a question that only the other person can answer? About which we can harbor no theory? And which, when the other gives the answer, she or he is the absolute authority, and we can't second guess the response? This is a fairly high bar in the quality of questioning.

I laughingly say," 'Don't you think it's George's fault?' is not a question, it is veiled judgment. 'Have you considered taking a different job?' is not a question. It is veiled advice." The rule: No advice, no suggestions of diets and books. Just completely open curious questions that only the other person can answer.

Softball Questions intrigue the mind, light it up, so the other person becomes engaged, not defensive. *Softball Questions* not only create a greater welcome for the other, they change our own internal stance, eventually moving us to genuine curiosity. These are questions that by their very asking move us to a place of curiosity, rather than judgment and analysis. We gain a real sense that we don't yet know what's going on here, but we are hungry to learn. And that we care for the other person finding a path forward.

I mention how difficult it can be to simply ask open, curious and generous questions. How challenging it is, particularly for leaders, to try not to "fix" the other person by offering advice, suggestions and lessons from their own personal experience.

How difficult it is to not have a back pocket theory about what is going on here. And to not fire off questions like news reporters on "Meet the Press."

None of these "fix the other person" approaches is particularly useful when a person is trying to sort something out, especially when the person must develop a workable solution that fits him and for which he must define his own next steps. Rather, with *Softball Questions*, we are asking questions that help the other person uncover his own internal wisdom. To sweep away the distractions that stand in the way of his moving forward.

To illustrate this I ask everyone in a group to think of a challenge, dilemma or quandary that is on their mind, that they'd like some insight on and that they are comfortable talking about with another person. After people have taken a couple of notes on the matter on which they seek insight, I invite them to practice their *Softball Questions* skills on me to make sure they have the idea, that they have the practice in hand. I choose a real dilemma for their practice knowing that my immediate reactions to their questions will make the case for the power of such inquiry.

The Art and Spirit of Leadership
judybrown@aol.com   www.judysorumbrown.com

Sometimes when I invite a group to practice their softball question skills on me, the result is startling, and immediate. The most memorable instant was when I offered my dilemma about my old car. I figured it was neutral enough and safe to share with them, and they could practice lobbing questions at me. I explained the dilemma: "I hate my car. It is ugly and lethargic, worn out, but still running."

"And I don't think I should go out and spend the money for a new car while this one is still running OK. But I sure don't like it."

There was a pause, then folks began to toss one question at a time at me, and I answered each naturally, without "editing." The first question: "What does a car mean to you?" I responded, "It's a way to get from point A to point B safely." Next question followed: "What matters most to you in a car?" I answered, "Safety, fuel economy." We were doing fine, and they clearly had the idea of open questions. I was pleased.

Then someone asked, "If you could have any car in the world what would you want?" My response was out of my mouth before I could stop myself: "A torch-red Mustang convertible!" I almost looked over my shoulder to see who had said that. I had. I, a Quaker, a conservative driver, a single mom, a driver of solid and sensible cars, without any extra money to lavish, had said, "A torch-red Mustang convertible!"

Then came the clincher question from a woman off to the side, gently and with curiosity: "What makes you think you don't deserve the car you want?" I don't know what I said in answer to that question, but I remember feeling as if some cog had shifted inside me. Somewhere.

When the class ended, I got in my old car, and soon found myself stuck in stopped rush-hour traffic on the north end of the Washington Beltway.

The Art and Spirit of Leadership
judybrown@aol.com   www.judysorumbrown.com

I hit speed-dial on my cell phone for a long-time friend, a Ford executive, who had for years encouraged me to buy Ford products: "Jim," I would say, "I don't have money for a new car."

Newly retired, he answered the phone. "Remember when you used to urge me to buy a Ford?" I asked. Delighted at my question, he asked, "What car do you want?" "A torch-red mustang convertible," I responded without hesitation. "Where are you?" he asked. "Stuck in traffic on the Beltway at 270," I responded. "When you get home there will be a pin number on your computer for the car," he said. "Just take it to a dealer, and they'll find you the car at a standard price and you won't have to negotiate."

Not all practice rounds end like that, thank Heavens. But I always make sure I offer a real dilemma for practice rounds, because only then can I respond authentically and can participants see the real impact of the questions. Only then can they notice the ways in which their own minds shift from certain to curious.

The surprise is that the questions have an impact not only on the person with the dilemma, but also on the person asking questions. At first we think we know what is going on with the person who has the dilemma. We have the answer. We just need to "sneak up on them with it." Then we realize this is much more complicated than we thought, and we don't have the answer. Then we realize that the other person's quandary isn't just theirs, it is in some odd way ours as well.

So when they have practiced sufficiently on me, I invite them to form threesomes and to take turns first with one person's dilemma and then the next. And using the "questions only" practice, explore what a difference the practice of curiosity and softball questions can make in opening insights within people.

The Art and Spirit of Leadership
judybrown@aol.com   www.judysorumbrown.com

An experimental mind-set for leadership

With all these practices to build curiosity, I am encouraging leaders to practice an "experimental mindset." I suggest they think of leadership as a setting for running small experiments. I suggest they notice the impact of their efforts, they learn from those impacts and then they adjust. Practicing an experimental mind-set can be as simple as paying attention to our assumptions and questioning them, or it can be as complex as the team-based "action learning process." Experimental mindsets are part curiosity, part the practice of wondering about how things work, and always about constantly testing one's assumptions.

Increasing our gentle curiosity about our thoughts

All these practices help us realize that our thoughts are not ourselves, they are just our thoughts. Somehow we have grown to think that if our thoughts are attacked, we are under personal attack. If we give up a thought, we are somehow giving up a bit of ourselves. The well-known "I think therefore I am" has somehow morphed into "I am what I think." But we are much more than our thoughts alone. Our thoughts today reflect just one possible framing of how things operate. Of the reality in which we swim. These practices above, taken together, remind us that our actions and intentions are not the only forces at play in the universe. This of course returns us to our earlier meditations on humility. Such a stance encourages life-long, unending, open and passionate curiosity.

Passionate Curiosity

The New York Times ran a story April 17, 2011, that caught my attention and has stayed with me. A review of *The Corner Office*, by Adam Bryant, began with notions about "passionate curiosity."

Many successful chief executives are passionately curious people. It is a side of them rarely seen in the media and in investor meetings, and there is a reason for that. In business, CEO's are supposed to project confidence and breezy authority as they take an audience through their projections of steady growth. Certainty is the game face they wear. They've cracked the code.

But get them away from these familiar scripts, and a different side emerges…they ask big-picture questions. They wonder why things work the way they do and whether those things can be improved upon. They want to know people's stories and what they do.

It's this relentless questioning that leads entrepreneurs to spot new opportunities and helps managers understand the people who work for them and how to get them to work together effectively. The words "passionate curiosity"…capture the infectious sense of fascination that some people have with everything around them.

This meditation on passionate curiosity makes me wonder if poets and CEO's have more in common than we would imagine: both practice the habit of relentless curiosity in order to see the world around them without the baggage of conventional thinking—their own and others.

The poet's mind

The poet's mind
rests free
of expectation,
or anticipation,
floating on
a sea of presence,
moment to moment,
a space of wonder,
curiosity and awe.
To be in such a place
requires that we
give up
notions we've been
carrying like baggage,
and just notice
what we see
traveling light
as newborns,
once again.

Judy Brown, January 28, 2009

The Art and Spirit of Leadership
judybrown@aol.com   www.judysorumbrown.com

Chapter Five

Create Open Spaces For Yourself and For Others

Often when I work with hard-driving executives, they mention the healing power of spaciousness in the way we work together. Many of us struggle to find space to think, to create spaciousness to absorb and reflect.

Spaciousness has many dimensions. It has to do with the nature of our attention, the way we experience time, the physical surroundings within which we work and the generosity of the welcome we create.

I have been aware in this writing of how many of the stories that have touched me, shaped my thinking and feeling, are stories about the wisdom of the stranger. The practice of creating open space for ourselves and for others also provides space that invites and welcomes the stranger to join us, and to speak openly, comfortably.

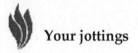 **Your jottings**

For me, the poetry that emerges is often the voice of an inner stranger, someone I must create space for in order to hear.

Heart songs

She'd sent one of her poems,
a powerful image
that she'd lived with
in her bones.

She noted that
I said I liked her poems,
but I never criticize them.

I thought of what she'd said.

It never had occurred
to me
that criticism
was what poetry calls for.

Like children of the soul,
the poems call for hugging,
to be held.
They're to be followed,
like one follows teachers,
or a guide.

It's not as if they're trees
we need to prune,
I thought,
but heart songs to be heard,
the children of our souls
singing their songs.

I only listen.

Judy Brown, November 11, 2003

The Art and Spirit of Leadership
judybrown@aol.com   www.judysorumbrown.com

Sometimes spaciousness is literal. It is physical, a matter of design. Is our meeting room spacious? Do we need to rearrange the furniture so it fosters the quality of exchange that we want? Is there natural light coming in and from several directions? Can we find ways to work in the natural world, the world outside our room?

Here Christopher Alexander, the philosopher of architecture provides insight and guidance. In *A Pattern Language*, Alexander illustrates practices, principles and patterns of design and architecture, with power and beauty at any scale, across all cultures, timeless. Alexander's book is known to an astonishing number of people in many disciplines. It has become influential not only in architectural circles, but also as a revolutionary work on how to think about design and scale, about space and the human experience, and at a most fundamental level, about what is satisfying to the human spirit. Those who own his book tend to pick it up again and again, leaf through it, underline ideas, circle the sketches—whether as an aid to building houses, creating meeting space for a rich conversation, thinking about the design of learning experiences, or simply to better understand the world around us in a richer way. Design matters.

This reminder that we are all designers or architects, whether we realize it, is a notion I first encountered in the work of Peter Senge. In an essay published in the *Sloan Management Review*, "The Leader's New Work," Senge frames leadership in three dimensions: the leader as lead learner and teacher, the leader as steward, the leader as architect. Always there is design at play in the work we do, acknowledged or not, intentional or not. I laughingly say that all good work starts with rearranging furniture, and there is literal as well as figurative truth in that notion. The literal dimensions: If we leave the physical arrangements as given, as we find them, then we will have the quality of thinking and conversation that we have always had. If we want a higher quality of exploration, and exchange, then we need to design to make it possible. To create space for it.

The figurative dimension of rearranging means we need to rearrange the furniture of the fixed notions in our heads.

I remember laughingly a day-long session on learning and sustainability that Peter and I and a colleague led. The room was beautiful with lots of natural light flooding the space, but by the time we were mid-way through the morning of our dialogue together, the sun was shining directly in our eyes. Each of us was coping differently with the too-bright light, until finally Peter said, "Let's turn the room around." And as a group we picked up every bit of furniture and turned it around, so the beautiful light was streaming over our shoulders and not shining in our eyes. I often think of the opening created by that phrase: "Let's turn the room around."

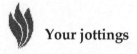 **Your jottings**

Design of process and space needs to include a place for solitude within the gathered community. A moment, a space, to think in quiet. To take a note or two about the questions with which we wrestle. Again, I am reminded of the speech by William Deresiewicz to the Plebes at West Point about the necessary role of solitude. A fragment of a poem of mine touches this notion, as well:

The Art and Spirit of Leadership
judybrown@aol.com   www.judysorumbrown.com

Trail

So write down words.
collect them,
hold them close.
Squeeze out the moments
like a sponge,
find solitude
to give them space....

Judy Brown, March 7, 1997

But, beyond matters of physical design, we have much more to work with in creating spaciousness. Listening itself creates open spaces.

My friend Mary Parish reminds us that, "Listening and waiting to talk are not the same thing." When I tell groups what she says, they almost always begin to laugh—because each of us recognizes ourself as that person "waiting to talk." The capacity to really listen to the other person, as Mary additionally counsels, to "Listen outside yourself," rather than listening to the inner dialogue we are running of what we want to say next, is essential in creating "open spaces" for others.

At the same time, in moments of solitude, practice listening to yourself. Give yourself the same respectful attention you might give a stranger. Set aside your need to judge whether the inner messages are relevant. Just listen. And in that listening, let all the dimensions of yourself find space for expression, exploration.

Create a welcome space, space that welcomes all of you. All the seasons of your life. That allows you to be where you are in your life. As you practice that spaciousness in your own inner space, it becomes natural to allow others the same spaciousness.

An important way to create spaciousness is to allow the seemingly paradoxical parts and points of view that you experience within yourself and others to be present, to be seen, to be heard. To stand beside one another.

Somehow when we allow for that diversity within us and around us, there can emerge a surprising sense of unity. To do so requires creating space that welcomes joy and sorrow simultaneously, that allows people to be where they are and to express where they are, without allowing one person's circumstances to silence another's.

Seasons

There are seasons
that we know will come,
inevitably, within our lives,
our families.
It helps that we have seen
the fall before,
the colors, falling leaves.
But in the season of the losses
yet to come,
we are not schooled,
nor skilled.
Each autumn is particular,
unique.
So ours will be:
the way the losses
pile like leaves
along the windrows,
and the winter of our grief,
and the spring in which
we come to life again,
ourselves,
and not ourselves,
changed,
changed irrevocably
and yet alive.

Judy Brown, June 22, 2008

The Art and Spirit of Leadership
judybrown@aol.com   www.judysorumbrown.com

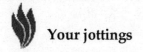 **Your jottings**

I remember a dialogue where the topics and the exchanges had been surprisingly open, varied, alive. It was full of silences, words, laughter, even tears. And at the end of our two days together, one member of the group, all of whom were part of a fairly formal and unemotional government organization, remarked with a sense of wonder, "Somehow you created a unity among us. By listening to all of us, and getting us to listen to each other, you created a unity among us. We never have had that here. Thank you."

Spacious listening and even generous silence can create closeness, unity among us. This notion is a challenge for leaders who often feel responsibility for saying something in order to create unity. It requires that one change a habit, develop a new practice of silence, acknowledge that the practice of listening itself creates unity. A colleague said of such practices, "They create psychological spaciousness." I think we long for such spaciousness.

However, this practice of listening to diversity, of creating open space, is not an easy one. We have a tendency to quickly put people in boxes, ourselves included.

The universe provides reminders of how we impoverish ourselves when we close our eyes to genius nearby because it is "packaged" in unexpected ways.

During a recent leadership program at the venerable Wardman Hotel in Washington DC, I saw a brass plaque on a pillar near our meeting room. It notes that the great African-American poet Langston Hughes served as a waiter at the Wardman and was "discovered" there by Vachel Lindsay, when Hughes waited on him. Why do people need discovering? Why are we surprised? Because we don't expect a waiter or bus-boy to be the poet who will change thousands of lives. Perhaps if we could just listen and notice with a spacious mind, we would discover such surprises everywhere.

Our current logic ("If this, then not that.") is a flawed logic. If a waiter, not a gifted poet. We do the same to ourselves. We say that if we are a teacher, salesman, clerk, waiter or a farmer we cannot also be a poet. And as poets, we forget we can also be teachers, executives, leaders, craftsmen. Each of us is so much more than we allow ourselves to acknowledge.

I so appreciated a colleague's recent musing that what had changed for her, and created such peace in her life, was that she no longer put herself in the "box" of her job, her work. She no longer found herself defining herself as a policy analyst, or an actress, or a graphic artist.

She let herself stay in the open space of a more whole and multi-facetted view of who she was. Carrying her newly-minted public policy degree, her love of the arts and theatre, she returned to the field of graphic arts with a sense of equanimity and without chafing against some self-defined rigidity she ascribed to the field and to her job. She found a new spaciousness allowing herself a more expansive self-definition. It is a space into which we need invite each other and ourselves.

The tendency to put myself in categories, in boxes, has been a constant challenge for me. I am perhaps more generous with others than with myself in this matter.

When I thought of myself as a farmer, I couldn't possibly see myself as a university administrator. As a Chief Financial Officer, I was unlikely to be a designer of leadership programs.

And then my favorite: If I am a serious executive and educator, what am I doing fiddling with words and writing poetry? How can I be a poet?

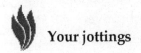 **Your jottings**

One day I was struggling with just that part of the "box"
thinking—agonizing about the place of my poetry in my life—the
bouquets of poems that have blossomed in my journal and that
have been such a confusing surprise and guide to me, and so
outside of the way I think about myself. A friend— a gifted and
oft-driven corporate leader— with whom I was having a quiet
dinner, responded to my worry about the poetry, with a simple
observation: "Maybe you are Leonardo." Those words startled me
and allowed me to see myself in a much more spacious way.

judybrown@aol.com   www.judysorumbrown.com

Leonardo

If I read
my poetry
out loud,
in public
am I then
a poet?

Not a farmer,
not a teacher,
not a focused
manager or
leader?

But a poet?

Maybe you are
Leonardo,
he said
quietly.

Judy Brown, August 15, 2000

Still, some days I forget that wisdom. If we can think more spaciously, and live more spaciously, maybe we can see that we are all like the multi-talented Leonardo Da Vinci. At once an artist, scientist, athlete, philosopher. But we hide from the implications of being Leonardo, perhaps afraid of what it might make possible in our lives.

If we could see Leonardo in ourselves and in everyone around us, a new expansive leadership practice would emerge. We would structure work and learning environments so others experience the open space to be fully who they are in all the rich and sometimes contradictory dimensions of themselves. The practice: listening and receiving. Listening and accepting. Setting aside judgment. Seeing that we are more than our job title. We are more than our to-do list.

Spaciousness in a world of task and focus

Spaciousness also requires being open to that which is seemingly not on our track, not among the things on our "to do" list— a paradox for most of us who must keep a running "to-do" list to maintain focus, to get the job done, to accomplish essential tasks, to get the work out the door, to keep track of things. My lists are certainly front and center in my life. Beside me at my desk. With me on my travels.

Then, last year, I decided even the to-do list can have some wonder, creativity and spaciousness in it. To make it a little more fun to attend to these necessities of life, I searched for something beautiful in which to keep my running "to do" list and found a lovely little book in an English village where we stay. It seemed to reach out to me, its cover beautiful in an unusual way, textured, with shades of gold and brown. I liked the look and feel of it when I ran my hand over the raised notations on the cover.

Only weeks later, looking more closely at the cover, and reading the tiny script inside that gave the source of the design, did I learn that the cover is a replica of Leonardo da Vinci's notes, observations and theories about the motion of water. Leonardo who was impossible to put in a box. Who kept notes on a subject that is all about flux and change—the motion of water. The book is a handy reminder to me that while the "to-do" list is useful, unfettered curiosity and spaciousness about things not on it can open paths to new and important worlds.

Remembering to suspend assumptions, judgment.

I have begun to realize that the practice of suspending judgment about myself and others is so central for me and to me, because of the limitations that judgment, particularly anticipated negative judgment, have had in my own life. Perhaps my habitual anticipation of negative judgment comes from my small-town Midwestern heritage and a sense that no matter where I have gone in life, the world seems smarter and more sophisticated than I am.

Perhaps it comes from having begun my schooling in a system that was by the measurements of the time "substandard:" We lost our school accreditation because we had no guidance counselor, a too-expensive luxury for our small system, which housed grades K-12 in a single building. So we were labeled "substandard." Later, when two of us in a class of 24 were named merit scholars (the highest percentage in the nation), we got our accreditation back.

Perhaps it is being solely a product of public education, even up through the PhD, in a world that places higher value on private schooling. Perhaps it is because I have fought against the idea that some abilities and some roles are exalted, and others not—a fight I have fought quite successfully out in the world, but much less successfully, I suspect in my own inner spaces.

The Art and Spirit of Leadership
judybrown@aol.com www.judysorumbrown.com

For all these reasons (and each of us has, perhaps, a unique set of reasons why we can't show up completely), I have found myself carrying secrets so that others wouldn't judge me, find me wanting and place limits on what I could do in the world. And I have subconsciously operated as if some callings were exalted and others not, despite the compelling wisdom of my mentor John Gardner on just that subject. Gardner wrote, and President Johnson quoted him:

> The society which scorns excellence in
> plumbing as a humble activity and
> tolerates shoddiness in philosophy
> because it is an exalted activity will
> have neither good plumbing nor good
> philosophy...neither its pipes nor its
> theories will hold water.

I often catch myself not accepting the spaciousness to be completely, openly, who I am, at the very time I am generous in granting others that spaciousness. Almost always it is because I fear the limiting power of the judgment of others.

The goofiest example of that pointlessly cautious behavior—keeping secrets so that others don't judge me— began when I was a freshman in college and persisted for decades afterwards. I tease myself about it to keep the lessons close.

It began with a summer job possibility that caught my eye: Pan American World Airways had a new program of recruiting a dozen or so college women, one each from 12 campuses, to serve as flight attendants in the summer and to be the on-campus recruiter at the placement center during the school year. It provided Pan Am some extra flight attendants in the summer and free recruiters during the school year.

At that time, Pan American was an international-only carrier, considered the US "flagship" airline. It sounded like fun; I was just nineteen and needed a summer job. Not withstanding the fact I'd only been on an airplane once in my life and the job was a long-shot, I thought it would be a great way to spend my summer. And it would pay well.

My mother had grave reservations about her only daughter, for whom she held very high aspirations, being a flight attendant, even for a summer. There were stereotypes of flight attendants that were far from flattering—that they were ditzes and of questionable morals—but I think Mom also doubted I'd get the job. So I applied. And to the astonishment of all, including me, I was selected.

I found myself in a remarkable situation for a college student: Trained in Miami as a full-fledged flight attendant, I joined the Teamsters Union (Pan Am was a closed union shop) and began flying back and forth from New York to Europe and the Middle East once or twice a week during the summer. I loved the work. I enjoyed the other women, mostly well-educated Europeans, with whom I flew. And having come from a tiny northern Michigan fishing village, I was suddenly traveling the world. Theatre in London. Escargot in Paris. Long walks in Rome. The bazaars of Tehran. Living in New York City with a group of Norwegian women who flew for Pan Am.

At the end of each summer, I would hang up my powder blue uniform (If you have seen the classic movie "Catch Me if You Can," you may recall the Pan Am flight attendants in this uniform walking arm in arm with Leonardo DiCaprio through the Miami airport), move back into my residence hall, resume my duties as a resident advisor, and go back to my school books. I did this for three summers.

But with graduation looming, I faced a difficult decision. I had been awarded a full fellowship for a PhD, which was a goal I held for myself. And although I longed to continue flying for just one more year before I went to graduate school, I was loathe to tell my graduate committee of my longing. In fact I had never told them about my unusual summer job at all. I was afraid that they would make the same judgment so many did about that job and the women who held it. Surely they didn't get PhD's. And certainly not on a full-ride fellowship.

So reluctantly, but necessarily I thought, I tucked my blue Pan Am uniform away in the closet, where it remains to this day, and started work on my doctorate. I told no one in the "professional side" of my life about that remarkable work experience. I feared their judgment might limit what I could do. I wasn't willing to take the risk.

Almost 20 years later, doctorate long finished and with a series of successful professional career moves behind me, my flight attendant background remained a secret. I was appointed Assistant Dean and Chief Financial Officer of what was at that time the largest business school in the nation with a faculty of more than 100. But as was true then, there were very few women; in fact, as I recall, there were only three women on that faculty. Including me.

One day, one of the other women faculty members came into my office for a signature on a financial document, and she spotted a plain blue bag beside my desk. It was a Pan Am flight bag with no insignia on it. While I knew I was breaking rules to ever carry a piece of flight uniform when I was not in full uniform, I'd taken to carrying my books in it. It was very handy and just the right size.

My colleague looked at the bag, and then she looked at me. "I have a bag like that," she said. "But it could not possibly be for the same reason you have a bag like that." Silence. "Why do you have a bag like that?" I asked. Her answer, after a pause, stunned me: "Because for four years before I went back to graduate school for my doctorate, I flew internationally for Pan American out of San Francisco." In a moment I realized that two-thirds of the female PhD's at the largest business school in the nation were former Pan American Flight Attendants. I decided that perhaps it was time to stop being so secretive and fearful about my past life.

In retrospect, I realize how many times my experiences in that job—experiences that bear on safety, on teamwork, on high levels of awareness—would have been useful to share at work. But I never mentioned them. Too risky. Too limiting. But more likely the secrecy and caution was what was limiting.

A man in one of my retreats once asked me, when I'd admitted giving up my journal writing for two or three years for fear someone would read it, "What's the worst that would happen if they knew who you really were?" That question remains apt.

My wise husband, now and again, slips me a piece of paper. His words to me: "If you don't value yourself as much as you should, surely no one else will. David E. Ward." The additional message I take from that is "value all of yourself."

So one dimension of spaciousness, within us and around us, is a freedom from judgment, the ability to stretch out completely, as fully as possible, into the person we are. Space to be. Space to think. Space to muse. Space to reflect. An invitation to be fully present. The wisdom to value ourselves.

At the heart of this spaciousness is a slowing down of thought. The discipline of changing the pace of our inner life. There are many meditative practices that strengthen that discipline. For me the journal and poetry have been the path.

Space of poetry

When you spend hours
in the space of poetry,
you learn to work
with shy words,
subtle words,
the notions that are needing
peace and quiet
to raise up their heads.
And so you lose the skill
of chasing after words
with Gatling guns of thought.
The mind grows soft,
relaxed,
sometimes near empty even,
waiting.
And the usual words
are sometimes hard to find—
the practical,
the names of persons,
towns, material things.
they disappear,
in waiting
for the
shy.

Judy Brown, June 15, 2006

The Art and Spirit of Leadership
judybrown@aol.com   www.judysorumbrown.com

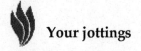 **Your jottings**

The power of physical learning

Spaciousness operates in many domains, including the physical domain. We can learn the practice in many ways, including through physical practice. One path of such learning for me has been martial arts. The leadership work of Aikido masters Richard Moon and Chris Thorsen has left me with a powerful and physical understanding of the spaciousness of real listening. Richard teaches executives the "seven second rule" — the practice of posing a question and simply letting it stand for seven full seconds, without adding to it, interjecting, or embellishing. Like the ring of a bell hanging in the air.

Seven seconds by the clock. Without reaction, inner or outer Sometimes seven seconds of silence. Terrifying for many of us who have the habit of moving quickly, filling in silences with our words. But that seven seconds is akin to the unmoving presence of great Aikido masters who, when faced with multiple assailants, seem barely to move.

Their waiting is a form of presence. Of practice. The seven seconds is a different form of disciplined temporal spaciousness and it allows people to consider the question, to think, and to then step into the space created by the question.

In most work cultures, however, such generous space is in short supply, particularly among the leaders. One day, working with a group of medical leaders on their dialogue skills, I described the seven second rule and its impact. The way it creates space for others to step in at their own speed, with their own wisdom. There was a long silence and then from the back of the room, one of the doctors began shouting, "You mean he's not an idiot? The guy isn't stupid? I thought he was an idiot." His colleagues, startled at the unexpected outburst asked him what he was talking about.

The doctor, who headed an emergency room in a hospital, began to describe his experience with a colleague who worked for him: "I ask him a question, and he just looks at me. So I ask it again a different way. He still says nothing. So I figure the question is too hard. I ask an easier one. Still nothing. Sometimes I just walk out of the room in disgust. I figure he's just an idiot." One of the other doctors began laughing: "He's not an idiot. You're hitting his re-set button every second. He never gets the time to answer the question you're asking."

Of course, there are many reasons a response may require spaciousness and time. It could be a matter of individual differences or style. Or it could be that the question is particularly powerful and the person needs a chance to absorb, to mull it over, before answering. Sometimes silence, like the silence at the end of a symphony in a great hall, is testimony to the power of what we have heard. The question needs nothing added, only the space and silence to be fully taken in.

One key to being comfortable with spaciousness is learning to love silence and solitude. That too is a practice, and one that takes discipline in this world of scattered attention, drivenness, constant noise and stimulation.

Insight into my own struggles, as an executive with a full life and a tendency to take on more than is rationally or humanly possible, emerged one early morning as I sat before a huge stone fireplace, in front of a blazing fire, writing in my journal. The poem that emerged from watching that fire has stood as a reminder to me, a single poem that somehow has traveled worlds on its own, bringing me requests for permission for its inclusion in books, poetry collections, articles, prayer books. That poem "Fire" seems to speak to people in all walks of life—including CEO's, scientists and religious leaders. Those who feel the weight of their responsibilities. And it daily speaks to me.

And while it has a surprising life of its own, the poem "Fire" is still at work in my own life, as I struggle with an habitual appetite for over-work. Perhaps the words I wrote those many years back are the best I can do on this subject.

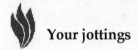 **Your jottings**

Fire

What makes a fire burn
is space between the logs,
a breathing space.
Too much of a good thing,
too many logs
packed in too tight
can douse the flames
almost as surely
as a pail of water would.

So building fires
requires attention
to the spaces in between,
as much as to the wood.

When we are able to build
open spaces
in the same way
we have learned
to pile on the logs,
then we can come to see how
it is fuel, and absence of the fuel
together, that make fire possible.

We only need to lay a log
lightly from time to time.

A fire
grows
simply because the space is there,
with openings
in which the flame
that knows just how it wants to burn
can find its way.

Judy Brown, November 18, 1995

Chapter Six

Practice Creativity and Hold Onto The Powerful Images That Emerge From That Practice

It has always seemed to me an odd thing about our culture that we operate as if creativity and artistry are the domain of a special few. The artists. We behave as if innovation and ingenuity are a peculiar, genetically-granted capacity awarded to others. But not us.

Poets are not us. Poets are other people who, as a British woman who wrote me with appreciation for the poem "Fire," noted are generally "people who spend their time swanning around." I was tickled by the British turn of phrase "swanning around." Floating serenely on the surface. Not engaged in the real work of life. She said she liked my poetry because it was about how to really get things done.

Her comment about "swanning around" reminded me of a participant in one of my retreats who, having read the poem "Fire," then watched me build a fire in the fireplace to prepare for a period of silent journal work. Later he said, with some astonishment, "You built the fire exactly as your poem suggests." "Of course," I said. "That is how you build a fire that takes right off from the start. It's a poem. But it's also a recipe for building fires."

Later the same man said thoughtfully, "You have the log-holder full of logs. Maybe you need a holder on the other side of the fireplace that you fill with spaces. Then you could put a log on the fire, and then a space. Next a log and then a space." His creative musing in that moment changed my life; now when I

judybrown@aol.com   www.judysorumbrown.com

pick up a log or a demanding piece of work, I am thinking about which "space" I am going to pick up next.

But it isn't only poets who suffer from a reputation of being out of touch. In our stereotype of artists as a different species, we think that musicians inhabit a different and unreal world, rather than composing a piece after leading a three-day retreat with corporate executives or after splitting a stack of firewood. And potters live an impoverished life at the end of a rural road, not going home after a long day as a Federal executive, and turning on the pottery wheel.

Yet perhaps each of us, in thinking about leaders who have brought special gifts to their work and have drawn talents out of us, may find to our surprise that many of those leaders have a history (or a sideline practice) as artists. Perhaps the person who inspired us had a serious practice as a musician, or was someone with a deep, lifelong practice as a dancer. Of course there are famous examples: President Bill Clinton and his saxophone; Secretary of State Condoleeza Rice and her early dream of being a concert pianist (When asked what her path was to becoming Secretary of State, she said, her first step was to fail as a concert pianist); President Eisenhower with his painting; and the Mayor of Chicago with his early training in dance.

Many of us actually have had our own experience with a leader-artist. I often ask executives to jot down the name of a leader whose influence has remained with them and to note specifically what that person's practices were that made such a difference.

One man described a leader who was clearly interested in his people as people. "How did you know he was interested in you as a person?" I asked him. He thought for a moment and said, "Well when someone was new to his team, he always invited them in to talk, to get to know them. Oh, yes, and he would say, 'And bring along a CD of your favorite music.'" The leader was

The Art and Spirit of Leadership
judybrown@aol.com   www.judysorumbrown.com

interested in the person as a person, and in what music spoke to them. Sharing his love of music with them, a creative dimension of himself seemingly unrelated to the work, was his way of welcoming the whole person and inviting their creativity into the game.

Wondering why it seems so clear to me that creativity, artistry and leadership are related, I began to ask myself how many of the people who shaped my thinking, created opportunities for me, opened unexpected doors, and were remarkable partners in successful creative endeavors were also artists. The answer is, a great many.

Perhaps the earliest experience had to do (not surprisingly) with poetry. My dad, like so many of his generation grew up reciting poetry. But he also read us poetry, and I remember most vividly his reading poetry to us from a wonderful leather-bound collection written by Clint Ballard. Ballard was Dad's boss, a man who served as a leader in the Cooperative Extension Service at Michigan State University. My own sense of poetry and its link to leadership, I now realize, was in part shaped by the expectation that somebody's boss could be a poet.

There were other artists who shaped my path as a leader. Gene Lawler, my Latin teacher and local school superintendent, was a jazz trombonist with a successful touring band in the years before he turned to a career as an educator. Bob Gluckstern, the physicist who headed the University of Maryland campus—who nominated me for the White House Fellows Program and named me to head his Women's Commission implementing Title IX—had a beautiful voice and was part of a prominent DC area symphonic choir. Rudy Lamone, saxophonist, was the business school dean who hired me as his unlikely chief financial officer and head of executive programs. With a "just do it" attitude, he had led a very successful jazz band until his late twenties when he turned toward college and a PhD in operations research—the tough math stuff.

The Art and Spirit of Leadership
judybrown@aol.com   www.judysorumbrown.com

One of the youngest and undoubtedly most innovative business deans of his time, he was a wonder to work with.

Betty Sue Flowers, poet and English professor at the University of Texas, later director of the LBJ Library, has been part of projects as diverse as Shell Oil's scenario building and Bill Moyer's work with Joseph Campbell. Every time we were in the same space, she would offer me some gentle observation or insight about her life or mine that always shifted my thinking in important ways. On one brief walk in the sunshine in Kalamazoo, Michigan, she told me she thought of me as a sunflower and that I needed to be more comfortable in being visible and in the sun. To not step back so much into the shade, out of public view. I was startled by her assessment, as I love being in the shade, but it made me reconsider my work and the place of my writing in that work. Betty Sue is an experienced leader, an innovator, a gifted writer and poet. And an out-and-out mystic. One who lives and works simultaneously in the worlds of spirit and action.

And another leader-artist who touched my life was Kerm Campbell, former CEO of Herman Miller, the western Michigan design firm, famous for the classic Eames chairs. Kerm, whose participation in choirs was central to his life, engaged me to develop a series of leadership seminars entitled, "Freeing the Human Spirit."

Max DuPree, an earlier CEO of Herman Miller, tells a memorable story about the millwright, a craftsman at Herman Miller, and a long-time employee. It's a story of unseen artistry.

The millwright had died and Max went to the man's home to pay his respects. As he entered the home quietly, he heard someone reading beautiful poetry. Curious, the CEO asked the widow whose poetry it was and she said that it was her husband's poetry. Max was shaken to realize that while he thought he knew the man and truly cared for him, he knew nothing of this dimension of the millwright's gifts.

Looking back over these leaders who helped shape my life and contributions, I now see a pattern of creativity not seen before. Just as Max DuPree hadn't been aware of the creativity in the millwright, I had not been conscious of the repeated pattern in my life of colleagueship, guidance and support from leaders who were also artists. I am aware how easy it is to miss the pattern of artistry in those around us, whose job titles suggest nothing of their creative gifts.

It has slowly become more evident to me that the capacity for creativity, like that for leadership, seems, by the evidence in my own life at least, to be widely distributed. And that capacity for creativity (often kept secret for fear of derision, or driven to the sidelines of our life by busyness) represents an important resource for our leadership. It is a resource in our own lives as leaders:

Artistry and creativity give us alternative ways of thinking, of approaching challenges. Artistry is a particularly important resource if we want our leadership to be innovative and transformational. But additionally, it is a resource because of the way it invites, even if unconsciously, the creativity out of those around us.

In my own work, as I have grown more comfortable in offering my poetry as part of my "practical" work in the world—teaching, coaching, leading—I am surprised at the number of (unlikely) folks who respond by sending me their own poetry. Sometimes it is their very first poem; sometimes it is a poem that is one of many that they have written but kept to themselves. Bankers. Engineers. Heads of power companies. Lawyers. Federal executives. Quiet poets, all. Slips of paper. E-mails with poems. Cards with their poetry.

When I was working in manufacturing plants, engineers would come to me and say, "I write poetry too. But don't tell anyone. Here's one I thought you'd like." I remember one three-day engineering gathering focused on dialogue and learning, that ended with my pockets full of bits of folded, crumpled paper— poetry passed to me—offered by friends and strangers alike. In secret.

So from all this experience, early and late, I offer words to capture the sense of how poetry (as is equally true of other creative practices), can wrap its arms around us and change our lives, and as an encouragement for all potential (and hidden) poets.

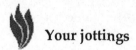 **Your jottings**

So write down words

So write down words.
Collect them.
Hold them close.
Squeeze out the moments
like a sponge; find
solitude to give them space.
Write on old slips of paper,
backs of check stubs,
grocery lists.
Use toll receipts
and paper towels,
old envelopes.
Find scraps of time
and scraps of paper.

Fill up your heart
by emptying yourself
of words; be graced by
giving everything away.
Reveal your self and
heal yourself by your own
generosity of heart and mind.

Judy Brown, March 7, 1998,
a fragment from a poem entitled "Trail"

The Art and Spirit of Leadership
judybrown@aol.com   www.judysorumbrown.com

My mentor John Gardner, a public-spirited leader and author of leadership books, used to say that there are talents, genius, and leadership everywhere. We only need to call them forth. Of course the first step in calling them forth is to believe they are there. Everywhere. In the most unexpected of places. Equally widely available, I believe, are artistic, creative abilities. And if Gardner says "call them forth," we remember Malcolm Gladwell saying that we must practice.

So our challenge is two-fold: to acknowledge the creative capacities within each of us. To call them forth. And then to pick up the disciplined practice of the form of artistry that we intend to practice and practice it.

This morning, as I am writing, I take a break and practice the piano. I am always learning, and there are lessons for me as an amateur at the keyboard — lessons about timing, about sound and silence, about major and minor key, about body-memory in the fingers that have played some of the same pieces for 50 years now, about carrying the thread of a melody through a complexity of other sounds. Hymns that I have played since I was 11 and became the pianist for the small Methodist church in my home town. Even "Rhapsody in Blue," my last recital piece, that leaves my arms and hands aching. Body memory. Insights deep within us. A way to remember that we are more multi-dimensional than we admit, and a way to become more whole.

Perhaps beyond making us more "whole," there is also a healing capacity in artistry, in craft. I am reminded that the words "healing" and "whole" have the same root word. So I think about healing and craft: Last year I returned to the practice of knitting after twenty-five years away from it. I had learned to knit as a 4-H club member when I was eight, and had remained an avid knitter until my daughter was born. Then, much more fascinated with her than the knitting (and she fascinated by the knitting and intrigued by the process of pulling the yarn off the needles), I set it aside. Temporarily I thought. Temporarily for twenty five years.

Then last year, wandering in the little rural town in England where my English husband and I take an annual holiday, I spotted a new shop tucked away. Back off the main street: "Nessie's Yarn and Knitting Shop." I was intrigued, so I poked my head into the tiny shop. There was Nessie, wan and frail, but smiling and welcoming amidst piles of yarn of all colors. Before I knew it I had selected beautiful deep rose wool for a scarf. Curious, I asked Nessie how she had come to open the shop. It had not been there the year before. Her explanation was a story of artistry, craft and healing.

Not long ago, she told me, she had had a massive stroke. It left her severely disabled, and the doctors gave up on her. She went home. There she sat. Unable to do anything. Finally, her sister said to her, "You can't just sit here and wait to die. Why don't you take up knitting again?" Nessie responded, realistically, "I can only hold a knitting needle in one hand." "No problem," said her sister, "You hold one knitting needle in your good hand, and I'll hold the other needle, and we'll knit together." That was the beginning of Nessie knitting herself back to health. She knit, and she knit and she knit. And then she opened her knitting shop which is remarkably always crowded with people. Sometimes one has to wait outside. And almost always, folks standing around tell stories of picking up knitting, again, after decades away from it. Because of seeing what Nessie has done.

Just this last week, on our annual English visit to stay connected to David's culture and his family, I poked my head into the shop. Nessie was still there. Looking a little frail, but full of life and smiles. So glad to see me, and I her. I asked her how she'd been. A rough spring, she admitted. Had pneumonia that put her in the hospital from February until April. She hated it. There were times when she thought she'd never get out. One day the doctor

The Art and Spirit of Leadership
judybrown@aol.com   www.judysorumbrown.com

said to her, "If you knit me a pair of socks, I'll have you out of here in a week." She did. And he did. And now she's back in the shop. Offering us a slice of her home-made chocolate cake, welcoming us back as if we were family. Is there indeed a longer life in the healing wholeness of artistry and craft?

I was fascinated by a recent obituary of a public servant, who retired from the government at age 96 and went on to live to be nearly 110. When asked his recipe for such a long life, he credited it to playing the piano, which he did all his life. His piano teacher said of his playing, well after age 100, "He has very young hands. When he starts playing the years fall away."

One of the assignments I regularly give to executives who are part of my work on creative leadership is to send them home at night with the task of picking up some creative activity that has meaning for them. It might be something they've always promised themselves that they would do.

I encourage them: "Perhaps tonight is the night to try your hand at that short-story you've had in your head. Or the scrap-book project that has been eating at you. Or picking out a tune on the piano, cooking that creative dish you've been thinking about, picking up a decorating project."

"Perhaps the thing you want to try your hand at is something you've set aside in the busyness of life: the camera that is collecting dust; the knitting in a bag in a closet; the piano that has moved from its status of musical instrument to serving as a fancy piece of furniture untouched by human hands; the woodworking project in the corner of the garage."

And I remind them that our check-in the next day will be about their experience with their creative homework. "Tonight," I say, "it is time to pick up that old guitar and practice." And despite people being a little bemused by the nature of the assignment,

158   The Art and Spirit of Leadership

generally they do their homework and return the next morning with intriguing reports on their experiences.

In one course, I had an unusual experience. After laying out all these homework possibilities on the first day of the two day leadership course and warning people that we would have a report from each of them the next morning on their homework, I was chagrined the next day when one of the executives was missing from class.

I thought to myself, "I guess I overdid it about the creative practice. She must have decided to just quit the course rather than do the homework." That had never happened to me before and I felt sort of bad about it. And I was surprised, too, as she had seemed quite engaged in our work.

Six months later, to my total surprise, the missing executive showed up for the second day of the same two-day course—of which she'd had only the first half months before. She was a stranger to the current group who had been given the usual first-day assignment: "Do something creative!" They were startled to see her. I certainly was.

"Ok," I said, "This morning, our check-in is about our experience with the homework. Who wants to go first?"

The missing executive's hand shot up. "I will," she said. "I suppose she gave you the same assignment she did with us six months ago," she led off. "You were supposed to do something creative?" People nodded.

"So let me tell you what happened to me. I did what she said. I went home and although it had been years since I'd worked on my pottery, I got out the wheel and tried my hand at it. To my surprise, I enjoyed it, and it was sort of relaxing. But that night I got a call saying I was to immediately start a new assignment, and

159   The Art and Spirit of Leadership

I never made it back for the second day of class. Still, I kept working on the pottery wheel. Pretty regularly."

"I didn't say anything to my staff about the pottery, but I guess word somehow got around. About ten days ago, I was headed out of the office at day's end, a bit earlier than usual. I told my deputy not to worry—I was taking work home with me so we'd be all set in the morning. 'I'd suggest you go home and do pottery rather than office work,' he said to me. 'Things seem to go better around here when you do that.'"

"So," she said, "I guess it's made a difference in my leadership."

You and I might surmise what the difference was in her leadership. Perhaps it was a changed sense of timing; perhaps she developed more of a sense of the "potential" in the human clay around her. Maybe she practiced a more engaged, "hands on" leadership. Perhaps she let up on her tendency to be a perfectionist. Only she and her colleagues might be able to tell us. But it was clear something had changed, and it was related to her practice with the pottery.

The leadership wisdom of pottery is at the heart of a classic leadership essay, *Crafting Strategy* written by the grand old man of strategy, Henry Mintzberg. Mintzberg, who is a powerhouse of strategic thinking, credits the wisdom of his wife, a potter, with helping him understand the importance of emergent phenomena. He describes circumstances where a glaze on her pottery cracks oddly and turns out to be a customer favorite, or an unintended design develops a great following among her customers. And he begins to incorporate into his own thinking, the importance of being open to the value of the unexpected.

But our potter executive is far from alone in experiencing a real impact of artistic practice on her leadership. These threads of artistry in our lives can have much to teach us, insights and lessons about timing, design, development and creativity that consciously or unconsciously can help us become wiser stewards of what we care about, of the work to which we dedicate our lives.

A woman who heads a life-care community spoke of the lessons she took from her long-time practice of making jewelry. "When I first started," she explained, "I looked for beautiful stones, and would put them together in a piece." "But over time," she said, "I could see that the more beautiful pieces were those that had a variety of stones, some eye-catching, some not, some large, some smaller, some beautiful, and others simply contributing to the general shape of things. It began to change the way I saw the people in my organization," she said. There was silence in the room as we absorbed that insight.

For me, the practice of writing poetry has helped me notice the small threads of imagery, the tiny idea that pokes its head up in the mind. I think I listen more carefully to the language of others; I hear their stories and I hope I hear them precisely. I know I remember them and they often come back to me at moments when they are of particular value, an important insight.

It also seems to me that my life as a poet has allowed me to become more comfortable with the unfinished, the oblique. I heed Emily Dickenson's poetic advice: "Tell all the truth but tell it slant." Sometimes laying something out in its unvarnished state doesn't help matters.

But it has taken time for me to learn to take my practice of poetry as seriously as I take my leadership work. When I wrote my first book, it was all prose and policy, concerning end-of-life decision-making, including my dad's personal story — except for three poems, some of my very first, that insisted on being in the book.

I sent a copy of that policy book to my favorite leadership and policy mentor, John Gardner, who as a cabinet secretary for LBJ

The Art and Spirit of Leadership
judybrown@aol.com   www.judysorumbrown.com

had shaped the Medicare and Medicaid programs and pushed through major civil rights legislation. I thought he would appreciate it as a serious piece of policy work.

His response was encouraging but startling. He told me he liked the book, and mostly he felt as if he had met my father through it and thought him a remarkable man. But, he said, "You are a poet, and you should be a published poet." I remember that moment: my heart sank, not because the praise didn't make my heart sing, but because somehow the hyphenated label "starving-artist" rang in my head.

But I took Gardner's words seriously, created a book of poetry and asked him to write the endorsement for it. He did. His endorsement on the cover of *The Sea Accepts All Rivers* reads:

> "Deeply moving…complex emotions and ideas are handled with disarming simplicity"
> John W Gardner, Former Secretary of Health, Education and Welfare

And years later, when we were corresponding about something else, he penned at the bottom of the letter, "I still believe every word I said about the poetry." He seemed to realize that it would take regularly repeated words of encouragement to keep me focused on my creative practice.

So I am relentless in my advice to executives that they should reintroduce artistry into their lives. I pepper people with ideas: Sketch. Soak up art. Pay attention to beauty. To nature. Read poetry. Don't have any poetry? Try these collections of poetry: *Teaching with Fire. Leading from Within.* Read Robert Frost (Which is the road less travelled by in your life?); William Stafford (What is the thread you follow that you have to explain?); Mary Oliver (What do you plan to do with your one wild and precious life?).

And then there are others: Billy Collins, Robert Bly, Emily Dickenson, or even closer to home, a poetry collection of mine, just published, called *Simple Gifts*. (I am shy even to mention it.)

Try singing. Don't panic, just start in the shower. Or the car when you are alone. Hum a little to start. It's all about rediscovering your voice. I tell them of my colleague Pamela Siegel who has returned to torch singing after years as a university administrator. Her musical practice is a serious matter in her life and involves studying voice and performing. In her work with teachers and executives, she leads them in rounds, giving everyone the experience of hearing their own voice in public. Hearing their voice next to others. Learning to hear others. Singing. Moving and singing. Pamela's deep personal study and practice with voice gives her the depth of understanding that allows her to engage others in the world of song easily and naturally, in ways that they might otherwise not experience. And through that experience, to develop their own awareness of timing, tone, tenor, harmony, dissonance and melody.

Still looking for ideas for artistry? Develop a photographer's eye for framing, composition, light. Practice playing with words; write tiny poems. Carve things. Build things. Play with words. Puns count. Design things. Play with objects. Learn the moves of dance and Aikido. Design a garden.

There are even playful exercises that step us into the world of movement and beauty. One of my favorites involves peacock feathers. I invite people up off their seats and out into an open area to experience the "creative tension" that artists live with — between the dream, the vision, the possibility (that's the beautiful tip of the peacock feather — the eye), and human limitations (that's where the "rubber meets the road — the bony tip of the feather). This also can help us explore the creative tension that leaders live with—between the vision, the goal, the possibility, and tough talk about current reality.

I give everyone a three-foot long peacock feather and invite them to balance it—first time, by putting the quill end on the tip of the index finger of their writing hand. And keeping their eyes only on that point—where the quill-end touches the end of the finger—to see how long they can balance the feather. This instruction is usually followed by a lot of laughing as they chase about trying to balance their feather with their eyes on the point, bumping into their colleagues, dropping feathers. People crouched over chasing the point. Lots of scrambling and laughing. We talk a bit about how that worked for them.

Then, round two. I invite them to again try the balancing, but this time to keep their eyes on the top of the feather, the "eye" of the peacock feather. And to see how they do. The room settles into remarkable silence, followed by an occasional, "Wow, that's really different." And we talk about how that is, and why they think it is so different.

We talk about how keeping our eyes on the top, on the prize, on the vision, makes it possible to see early shifts in the feather that we naturally adjust to—without having to think about them. We notice that we can move without slamming into our colleagues because our range of peripheral vision is much greater. And we note, as one young woman explained, that it is easier because "It is so beautiful. The eye of the feather with its lustrous green and purple is so beautiful. It is a joy to look at it." Although creativity takes many forms and expressions, it reminds us of what is most beautiful, what matters most. It connects us with the beauty that we have often lost sight of and with our role in creating that beauty.

I tell people about my friend Arawana Hayashi's work in collaboration with Otto Scharmer's exploration of innovation: the

The Art and Spirit of Leadership
judybrown@aol.com www.judysorumbrown.com

U theory. The U theory sketches the process of innovation as: sensing, letting go, letting come, prototyping. Arawana's life-long dance and movement practice is rooted in the seemingly distant world of 7th century Japanese court dance and the contemporary practice of street theatre and social presencing theater. She brings to her work with executives the depth of her movement training, encouraging them to experience space and spaciousness in totally different ways. She guides them to become increasingly aware of their own movement, of what she terms "Embodied Presence: The Art of Making a True Move."

Embodied learning makes a difference. When I am working with leadership programs that include an innovation project, or an action learning project, and I think a change of pace will be helpful, I often move people out of our meeting room into a larger space—an atrium or hallway. And into action.

I say to them: "This is a chance to think about how we approach change, and goals, and innovation. Without using words. This is a no words exercise. So here is the deal: Without letting anyone know, I want you to identify a spot on one of these walls that represents an important goal to you, or an innovation or change you are pursuing. When I say 'go' and the music starts, I want you to head with real determination for that goal."

So I start the music (music helps them move to a uniform beat— ABBA is good for this), and shout, "Go!" and off they go. Crashing into one another. Determined.

"OK," I say, "How was that?" They laugh and talk about their colleagues who are in the way of their "innovation goal," the person who insisted on standing in the space of their goal, the chaos of it all. Often like things at work.

"OK now, round two," I say. "This time, mentally select a different spot on the wall to represent the innovation. Have you

165

got it in mind? This time, when I start the music and say 'go', I want you to hold the goal in the 'back of your mind' and just move toward openings that seem to get you going in the right direction."

Again, the music. And "Go!" The crowd dissolves into a remarkable "flow" of people weaving among others, creating room for each other. One man stands quietly and begins moving only after everyone else has moved away, leaving him a clearing.

"And how was that?" I ask. "Remarkably different." Music and movement and indelible insights about innovation, goals and change.

Not all of the lessons we find in the world of artistry require an expert's knowledge or some group experience. Sometimes all it requires is your own curiosity and paying attention.

Once a friend and I were lured by curiosity to an exhibit of the paintings of Grandma Moses, the famous American primitive landscape painter. For those of us who consider ourselves late-bloomers in our artistry, or who approach our art with no formal training, Grandma Moses is an inspiration: She took up painting in her 80's when her arthritis got too bad to continue working with needlepoint. She continued painting until she was well past her 100th birthday.

My friend and I looked at one after another of the artist's paintings. We were particularly intrigued by her last canvas, completed shortly before she died. Wanting to learn more about her, we watched a video of an interview by the famous tough, chain-smoking reporter, Edward R. Murrow. The poem that follows tells the story: Here indeed is an experience with the mystery of artistry. And the potential to continue learning from the practice of art, for as long as we live.

Grandma Moses talking with Edward R. Murrow

"How do you paint?" he asked her.
She was 95 years old,
painting trees onto a nearly finished
New England landscape,
her standard medium: masonite,
covered with two coats of white paint.

"I paint down" she said.
"I start with the sky,
and then do trees,
and then the ground.
I paint down."

He looked like he expected
something more complicated
in response.

"And why, Grandma Moses,
have you never painted
anything from the Bible?"

She continued painting the trees.
"There's a lot unknown
about the Bible. You don't
paint what you don't know."
She went back to painting trees.

The Art and Spirit of Leadership
judybrown@aol.com   www.judysorumbrown.com

The last painting that she did,
when she had passed her century mark,
was a familiar country scene,
this one, alone among the many,
had a rainbow.

My friend and I stood looking at it
for the longest time. Held somehow by the
knowing that it was her last. My friend said
"Look, how the top band of the rainbow,
seems to pull free and rise through the sky,
beyond the frame and out of sight".

You only paint what you know.

Judy Brown, June 3, 2001

The Art and Spirit of Leadership
judybrown@aol.com www.judysorumbrown.com

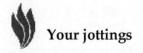 **Your jottings**

The Art and Spirit of Leadership
judybrown@aol.com www.judysorumbrown.com

The lessons of the creative process can help us hold onto life's lessons in lasting ways. Perhaps that's why, over the years, I've taken to giving my graduate leadership students a lot of running room with their final papers. And encouraged them to consider a non-traditional form for the final project. It's traditional that a final paper in a graduate course is carefully researched, well argued, and generally about 25 pages in length. "Single or double spaced?" always comes the question. Quoting Abraham Lincoln's quip in response to the repeated question of how long were his legs, my answer: "Long enough to reach the ground." Laughing.

Too often the academic tone of the paper strips the student's voice from the pages and, like so many projects, the student does the work, turns it in, receives a grade, and never looks at the paper, or thinks about it again.

But my reason for teaching leadership has been to encourage people to create a leadership framework, an understanding, that will be reflected powerfully in their lives for years to come and will sustain them in their leadership and their learning. That is a quite different task. And so I say, "While you may want to do the traditional paper, you could also explore a different and creative format." So over the years I have been handed wonderfully creative projects—that have stayed with me, and I suspect with the students. They have included

- An architectural sketch of a village with the various buildings representing the ideas and leadership frameworks that we touched during the semester—a sketch that ended up being the inspiration for my first website.
- A beautiful artistic journal detailing a student's journey to understanding.
- A photographic representation of travels and interviews with leaders.

The Art and Spirit of Leadership
judybrown@aol.com www.judysorumbrown.com

- A 6x8 foot quilt that captured the core ideas about leadership that the student wanted to always hold to—and that she intended to hang on her office wall. "That should start good conversations," she said.
- A letter to an unborn child.
- And the paper beginning with James Thurber's story of "The Unicorn in the Garden"

Artistry and nature

I often invite people to experiment with what the natural world can suggest to them about important matters in their own lives.

The guidance I provide is simple: "Take your journal outside with you and find something in nature that catches your attention, something that 'speaks' to you. Sit with it. Observe it. If you wish, sketch bits of it. What images, words does it suggest? Jot them down. Are you wrestling with some difficult change? Take some notes on how the natural thing deals with what you are dealing with."

Off people go with their journals. The first time, probably thinking to themselves that this is goofy. Yet I remember the first time I was sent out on such an exploration—by Paula Underwood, the Native American leader and educator—I returned with an entirely different take on what was troubling me. And some simple sketches that were eye-opening.

Remembering my own bemusement about the assignment the first time, I was caught off guard by the appreciation of a Texas executive group after the assignment. Their thoughtfulness about what they observed indicated they actually enjoyed the process of sitting with their "natural thing." A month later when we gathered again, I was startled when one of the executives took me aside and said, "We're wondering when we get to go sit with our 'natural thing' again. We are going to get to do that again, aren't

The Art and Spirit of Leadership
judybrown@aol.com   www.judysorumbrown.com

we?" I had not planned on repeating it, but the question changed my thinking. So thereafter, the visit to the natural thing was part of the work each time we gathered.

Why is it so powerful to simply "be" with something in nature? To observe without judgment? Frederick Frank urges us to sketch it not as we think the object is, but as it actually is, looking only at the thing and not at our sketch. I think that once we see the natural thing before us with such fresh eyes, we see people with the same fresh eyes, appreciating their nature as well. And then perhaps later, we see ourselves in a new and natural light.

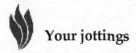 **Your jottings**

One of the Texas executives, after sitting by the dried-up river bed near our conference center, said something to me that prompted this poem:

Big flood

"Big flood,"
he said,
Sitting by
the dry river bed,
mulling over something
stuck at work.
"Big flood come through
wash all the crap out,
clean it out."

Later he said,
quite quietly,
"It's not the season."

Judy Brown, November 17, 2006

The Art and Spirit of Leadership
judybrown@aol.com   www.judysorumbrown.com

Last spring, in the midst of numerous changes in my life, I found myself fascinated by the hidden wonder of a deep purple French lilac which I discovered near my family's old Northern Michigan cottage. The lilac had likely been planted around the turn of the last century, about the same time that the old cottage was built, perhaps around 1910. For decades, hidden in the overgrown shrubs along the road, the lilac worked to find its way to any ray of sunshine. Crawling along the ground. Tangled. Doing the best it could with where it found itself.

We were stunned to see the great grapelike blooms dangling here and there in the underbrush. Carefully my husband and I lifted it up, realizing we couldn't move its limbs too far too fast without breaking something. But loving its beauty, we slowly, gently helped move it toward the light and propped it up with an old two-by-four and a length of rope. Simply being with, appreciating and working with that boney old bush carried lessons for me.

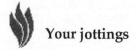 **Your jottings**

The Antique Lilac

Bit by bit
we lift it
back into the sunlight.
It's grown
for years
hidden and bent,
crouching
along the ground
beneath the tangled pines
down by the road.

(Until last year
I didn't know
that it was there at all.)
So in my decades
here, in this my
cottage homestead
on the lake,
it's grown in darkness,
blooming
against the odds.
Unseen.

Now rediscovered,
it's a mad profusion
of huge grape-like blooms
heavy and rich, deep purple,
hanging high in sunlight
where we've propped it
with a clothesline pole

judybrown@aol.com   www.judysorumbrown.com

made of a two-by-four,
and resting on a rope
between two trees.

It fairly shouts of beauty.
If it could sing,
it would sing opera
and you would hear it
clear across the lake.

One has to meet it,
such a twisted,
tangled thing,
where it has grown
over the years,
and move it gently,
carefully
toward the light—
A hundred year old lilac
doesn't invite
sudden change—
It needs encouragement and space,
time and support,
to grow into the light
from which it first
took root.

Judy Brown
Michigan, May 17, 2010

I am reminded of Arthur Ashe's words of wisdom near the end of his life: "Start where you are. Use what you have. Do what you can." For me, the lilac carries lessons about potential and persistence, about change and encouragement. And about the importance of allowing time.

It reminds me of the time, years back, when a friend who headed one of the most visible government statistical organizations, stopped me in the hallway of our Federal agency and said, "I wanted to tell you something that happened to me last week. Somehow I think you would want to know about it." She explained that she had taken a week off to help her father pack up his home in Florida so he could move into a smaller place. She, accustomed to running a huge organization where things got done "snap, snap" on a disciplined schedule, found her father sitting motionless on a box in the hallway, after everything had been taken out of the house. She urged him to get into the car. He just sat. Finally he said to her, "Not everybody moves as fast as you do." His words have stayed with me.

The practices of creativity, particularly noticing the pace of nature, can help us hold onto insights and perspectives we would otherwise lose sight of. If we have a creative practice, we soon see that it can help us identify images that matter to us, that speak to us, even images that simply capture our attention, when we don't even know why, at least not yet.

As a path to that increased awareness of imagery that captures our attention, I often shift groups from words to pictures. The practice is simple: a practice of using pictures, often seemingly unrelated to the issue on their mind, to prompt insight. The most widely known resource for this process is the Visual Explorer (a set of more than two hundred 8 ½ x 11 pictures available through the Center for Creative Leadership), but sometimes I use my own collection of pictures assembled over the years.

The Art and Spirit of Leadership
judybrown@aol.com   www.judysorumbrown.com

I encourage others to start such a collection on their own. The process of working with the pictures is revealing and fun in and of itself. Lighthearted.

> I invite people to make some notes in their journal about an issue or dilemma that is on their mind—something that is important to them, about which they would welcome some new insights, and that they would be willing to talk about with two other people.

> After everyone has made their notes on their issue, I have them share their thoughts about that issue briefly with two partners. Sharing just enough so the partners have a sense of the dilemma. Sitting in three-somes, knee to knee.

> Then I invite everyone to wander in silence among the 250 or so pictures that I am scattering on the floor. I ask them to pay attention to which pictures attract their attention—there doesn't have to be any logical reason for the attraction, nor any link to the issue they've taken notes on. They should just pay attention to when a picture seems to reach out to them. Pick up that one, but continue looking at others; another might intrigue you more, and if it does, swap the one you are holding for that one. For about five minutes in complete silence, people walk among the pictures, picking up one then putting that one down for another that appeals to them more.

> Then people return to their partners with their chosen picture in hand. I ask them to spend a few minutes in quiet, taking notes in their journals about their picture: what it is a picture of, what drew them to it, what strikes them about it. Then the three, round robin, introduce their picture to their colleagues. When the first person has finished "introducing" her picture, she is then invited to explore out loud with her partners any links that she sees

to the dilemma on her mind. There may or may not be any that strike her. When she is done, the partners are invited to share any reflections they have—noting that if they had her dilemma, one link that might have struck them would be.... That particular framing gets folks out of "psychoanalyzing" each other and into sharing, each from her own perspective.

Then person number two introduces her picture and after the introduction invites reflections from her partners. (I use the term "introducing" the picture, because it so clearly signals that the person holding the picture is the one "in charge" of this part of the conversation.) And person number three follows the same pattern.

Sometimes, as a way of further stretching minds and taking insight not only from what we choose but from what life "deals" us, I use an additional technique called the "wild card": Having kept a stack of pictures out of the "deck" that I had spread on the floor, I pass out a "wild card" face-down to each participant with the instruction, "Don't peek." Then I ask everyone to turn over her wild card in silence and take notes about the picture and her reaction to it. "What stands out for you, what strikes you? Does it appeal to you? Is it repulsive? And is there any insight from this picture about your dilemma?"

When everyone has taken notes, I invite each person to introduce her "wild card," note any links to the dilemma, and again, to invite her partners' insights as well.

This process offers a chance to be reflective, yet in a relaxed, playful and mind-stretching way. And it introduces the process of learning from images, particularly from "unrelated" images, stretching our mind and our creativity. And most importantly to me, it allows participants to practice being the "authority" on their own picture, to be creative in the possibilities it offers them.

For me, the images of transformation, innovation and change are particularly important, perhaps because I am always trying to figure out the nature of transformation, change and innovation. So, I look for those images in the natural world.

The natural world does change really well and all the time. I watch the seasons and the tides. I watch the trees go through winter and come out the other side in limey, leafy green. I notice the way the daffodils poke their blooms up through the snow. Year after year. I notice how the surface of the river changes moment to moment, and how, if I study it, I can learn to recognize the presence of otter simply by the pattern of her wake on the river. I think about the lessons of nature for myself.

This morning I watched a pair of huge, fluffy, white tundra swans swoop down upon the creek out front, not realizing that what seemed like open water was skimmed over with a thick skin of ice. The first of the pair slid across the ice, webbed feet out like brakes, and landed finally in a small bit of water. From that small pool, he began operating like an ice-breaker, swimming hard into the ice ahead, creating an opening, backing up again, ramming the ice again, until he had created a path to open water near where a stream comes into the creek. The second swan serenely followed the first, floating swan-like, gracefully.

I watched this process for many moments, realizing that I may wish to see myself as akin to a graceful and peaceful swan. But, there are moments when I must shift to being an ice-breaker so that others can follow me. Without my practice of poetry, the moment would have been lost on me, as would the lesson about my leadership.

180   The Art and Spirit of Leadership

No seed grows

No seed grows
except by
breaking through
it's own
protective coat.

Judy Brown, March 24, 2005

The Art and Spirit of Leadership
judybrown@aol.com   www.judysorumbrown.com

For most of us, stepping into the arena of artistry and creativity is challenging because of the judgments we hold about how imperfect our efforts, how poor our performance. I remember the poet Robert Bly telling me of a conversation he had with fellow poet William Stafford. Stafford had had a practice, for decades, of getting up each morning and beginning his day by writing a poem. And he was urging Bly to do the same. "But Bill," said Bly, "What if it's a lousy poem?" Stafford's response: "You just have to lower your standards." Often when I am experimenting with something new, or when I am letting a poem show up as it wishes, I think of Stafford's words: "You just have to lower your standards."

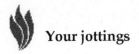 **Your jottings**

In that sense, the practice of art or craft is a practice of courage, of being willing to be less than perfect, of letting new fresh notions far from finished in form, see the light of day. A lasting lesson about that courage and about the need to remember our great masterpieces as well as the efforts that are far from perfect comes from my Maine potter friend Carole Beal:

Seconds

She sells the perfect ones,
the cups and bowls without
a flaw, the ones that
with a potter's eye and hand
she knows will likely never
chip nor break,
will stand the heat and cold,
weather a thousand washings
and remain as new.

The seconds?
Those she keeps and uses,
lives with day to day.
Some have a flaw
that even I can see;
others look perfect
to my untrained eye,
but she's aware
they won't withstand
the challenge
of a stranger's
daily use.

The Art and Spirit of Leadership
judybrown@aol.com   www.judysorumbrown.com

"Incomplete ideas" she calls
the ones she keeps
just for herself.
"Unfinished thoughts,"
the seconds, plates and bowls,
not flawed but incomplete.

Perhaps it's true for
all of us who craft a thing,
who write a poem,
build a boat,
shape an idea
or an enterprise.

The perfect ones,
the ones that work,
we sell or give away.
We move beyond them,
onto something new.
They pass out of our minds.

The yet unfinished thoughts,
ideas incomplete,
things that won't work,
we look at every day.
We live more with the
flaws of craft
than with its perfect form.

Perhaps that's why
it's difficult to see
the grace of our own artistry,
to bring to mind the gifts
we've shipped away from us,
to recollect the beauty of
a plate that someone
else can touch
from day to day,
while we ourselves
thrice daily
take our nourishment
from pieces that
we know are flawed.

Judy Brown, November 19, 1997

The Art and Spirit of Leadership
judybrown@aol.com   www.judysorumbrown.com

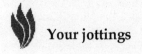 **Your jottings**

Chapter Seven

Expect To Find Gems, Gifts and Genius In The Most Unexpected Packages

To foster the belief that talent is hiding everywhere, often in plain sight, requires a practice of allowing ourselves to be surprised by the gems, gifts and genius that life presents. Surprises.

Sometimes those surprise packages are people. Sometimes they are life experiences.

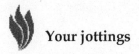 **Your jottings**

The Art and Spirit of Leadership
judybrown@aol.com   www.judysorumbrown.com

Gifts

What are the gifts
we have,
unused,
packages laid out
before us,
treasures still un-treasured,
completely overlooked?
Our life is less at risk
through violence,
disease,
and accidents,
than through our inattention
to the gold
life's river
washes clear each day.

Judy Brown, November 24, 2008

Always the gifts are unexpected. Sometimes we are startled by them, shocked. Sometimes the surprise challenges our deeply held assumptions about how the world operates.

Welcoming surprise is key. And challenging. I think of how many leaders and managers pride themselves on a maxim, often engraved in brass and placed upon their desk: "No surprises." As if success, personally and organizationally depends on ensuring predictability.

Yet when I invite people to jot down the stepping stones that have led them to where they are in their life and their work and to have a quiet conversation with one or two others about what they see in their notes about those stepping stones, they almost always talk about surprises. How their life has been shaped by the unexpected, welcome or not.

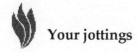 **Your jottings**

The Art and Spirit of Leadership
judybrown@aol.com   www.judysorumbrown.com

Story lines

Some time back,
the story-line
we had in mind
disappeared
into some brambled place.

And we were left
beset by our anxieties
about where the path
had gone,
wondering with our feet,
as still we edged along
into foreign terrain
that has an odd appeal
as it turns out:

Unexpected joys,
created out of
mutual confusions;
and grievings shared and hidden,
creeping out of what
never came to be
that we had counted on;

The Art and Spirit of Leadership
judybrown@aol.com www.judysorumbrown.com

strange stories
that we used
to guide us;

myths that promised
trails we never found;
and improvised stories
that grow out of the
gifts and tragedies
of a life
we never had expected.

Judy Brown, November 3, 2002

The Art and Spirit of Leadership
judybrown@aol.com   www.judysorumbrown.com

Spotting talent in the world around us requires a powerful openness to surprise. A delight in the unexpected. Enjoying the surprise. Often the unexpected gifts show up very close to home or in the voice of the very young.

When my daughter Meg was about 12, I was driving her to school, my mind on the day ahead, thinking of my to-do-list. "Mom," she said. "Look at those people walking up that street." "I can't, Meg," I said, "I'm busy driving." "Just peek," she said. I glanced up the street and saw three perfectly normal people walking along. "So?" I said.

"It just occurred to me that those people have lives of their own." she said. "They aren't just characters in my drama."

I nearly ran off the road. From the passenger seat of my car, an echo of Martin Buber's "I-thou" concept. And an echo of a thought-provoking book often recommended to me by leaders, called, *Leadership and Self-Deception*. The book could well be summed up in the words of my 12 year-old daughter: "Those people have lives of their own. They are not just characters in my drama."

It takes practice to slow down enough to take in the surprise, (I almost missed the chance to hear from my daughter—how many other chances have I missed, I wonder.) And it takes further practice to delight in it. The delight is often the hardest part.

When Thomas Kuhn, American historian and philosopher of science, led scientists through a simple experiment that would help them understand that they didn't see things as clearly as they thought, the scientists didn't "get it." They didn't welcome the surprise. They just got mad at Kuhn. Not all people, particularly those who set a high value on their expertise, have the practice of delighting in surprise.

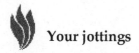 **Your jottings**

In our "report suspicious behavior" culture, it is hard to hold in mind that not all surprises are bad ones. Although some are. We seem to have schooled ourselves to live with our knees flexed and our head down ready for anything bad. When on September 11, 2001, my brother called me from rural Michigan to make sure I was OK (we lived inside the Washington Beltway and my daughter attended school next door to the highly visible National Cathedral) he ended the call with "Well, keep your eyes on the skies." And I don't think he was suggesting watching for beautiful sunsets.

That painful day was one of bright blue skies. And we still have beautiful sunsets. But these days our eyes seem squinty, wary. Our anxieties multiply. Air travel seems particularly prone to those anxieties:

Flights

Yesterday,
an easy flight
for me. Not so
for him.
He was an hour
late because a
jar of caramel sauce
inside a suitcase, broke,
and ran out, down
the outside
of the plane.
They didn't know
what the suspicious
liquid was.
Was it mechanical?
A terrorist plot?
As it turned out
they should have
called for ice cream,
not mechanics
and the bomb squad.
So hard to know
what we are seeing,
sometimes. Especially
when we're scared.

Judy Brown, August 23, 2010

The Art and Spirit of Leadership
judybrown@aol.com   www.judysorumbrown.com

The notion of not being able to see clearly because we are used to the "usual" way of seeing bears on the way we see leadership itself. I notice the language in a story from the *Washington Post*: "The popular uprising in Egypt triumphed Friday as President Hosni Mubarak surrendered to the will of a leaderless revolution and stepped down after 30 years of autocratic rule over the Arab world's most populous nation."

The Washington Post, hardly noticing its own framing of the change, is caught in its traditional view of leadership as being what a single person with the title of leader does: the notion of a "leaderless revolution."

"Leaderless?" Who were the people who began this movement toward liberation by reaching out on the Internet? Who were the people who day after day risked their lives and their livelihoods on change? Who stood, and marched and camped in the streets? Who were the military leaders who said they would not use violence on the demonstrators? Who were the lawyers and doctors and teachers who marched in the streets?

"Leaderless?" I don't think so. But because we have schooled ourselves to believe that the practice of leadership is a "solo" undertaking, we, like the *Washington Post*, have a hard time recognizing collective leadership over time. Because the power and energy came from many sources, seemingly from everywhere, it seemed to the customary way of thinking, that it came from "nowhere." It was in that sense, an unexpected "surprise." Which delighted some and dismayed others. And was invisible to many.

This contemporary political story is an echo of the forest service in France seeing the reforestation that Jean Giono's shepherd initiated as a "spontaneous regeneration of a forest." Our major media see the determined work of thousands to bring about change as a "leaderless revolution."

195

We work within limitations created by our usual ways of seeing, of thinking. Often embracing the surprise means giving up control over something we like to think we control. And sometimes, for me, the most powerful, and embarrassing examples of limited thinking, are close to home.

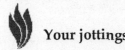 **Your jottings**

Christmas

She wanted pearls,
long strings of pearls,
draped on the tree.

But I dismissed
her plan, said
we had not
enough of them
to lavish on
the tree.

This was my
perfect tree
just as it was
without the pearls.
I didn't listen
to her heart.

I didn't have the
spirit that could
hear her childish
wisdom for my life.

A tree for two
is quite a different
tree; a family tree
has difference that's
woven in its limbs.

The Art and Spirit of Leadership
judybrown@aol.com www.judysorumbrown.com

This morning
I got up
and in the dark
I looped long strands
of pearls
most carefully
upon my perfect
tree.

It was more
beautiful by far
than it had any
right to be,
more beautiful
because her presence
and her clarity
(and also pearls)
had made it so.

Judy Brown, December 9, 1998

We each very likely have parts of our life where we are most likely to be wary of surprise. We therefore overlook the gifts and gems that life offers us. For me, it takes discipline to stay open to life's surprises. And so my Christmas poem stands as a constant reminder of how set one can become in ways of thinking, how immune to the gifts, talents and perspectives of others.

My favorite way to practice being delighted by surprise is to watch the first audition of the pudgy, crooked toothed Welsh car-phone salesman Paul Potts, as he steps out, terrified, onto the stage of "Britain's Got Talent." Paul has explained that "Confidence has always been a bit of a problem for me. I've always had a little difficulty being confident." That is more than evident as he readies to sing a few lines from the aria "*Nessun Dorma*." But within seconds, his glorious voice brings tears and wild applause from the audience and judges. It will eventually bring him a chance to sing for the Queen.

But as his last notes in this first audition fade away, so does his extraordinary presence, and he sinks back into the uncertain, unglamorous car-phone salesman role. Once again unsure of himself. Unaware of the impact his remarkable performance has had.

Each of us is, in our own way perhaps, like Paul Potts, unconvinced of the power of our own gifts. And each of us as a leader, needs to realize that Paul Potts is everywhere around us — hidden talent, uncertain of its value, shy about being seen, having a little difficulty with confidence. Our belief that unexpected talent is possible, indeed everywhere, is a critical leadership practice.

Recently, a group of community officials from around the state of Maryland and I were in a dialogue about local leadership. Together we watched a recording of Paul Potts' unexpected performance. Later one of the women took me aside, a local leader who serves one of our smaller communities. She explained how difficult it was for her to complete the written assignment for our work. She had no confidence in her ability to write. "I am Paul Potts," she said to me quietly. Enough said.

My most recent reminder of how we can be surprised by the power of the unexpected comes through in the words of a mid-career student, a former military man, who was so quiet in class that I felt, to my embarrassment, that I barely knew him.

In his final paper about leadership, he shared a story of being surprised by life, and in doing so, surprised me:

> In 2005, after a lot more time in the military than I ever planned to serve, I left the Navy. To my surprise, somebody wanted to hire me, and I moved to the UK. After a couple of months of living in North Yorkshire drinking English Ale and doing my best to only work 40 hours a week, I found that, after years of deploying and going a million miles an hour, I was really uncomfortable not working all the time. I was used to going nonstop and I wanted everyone to work long hours with me.
>
> Fortunately, one day I found a book that would have a pretty profound effect on me. The book was Alfred Wainwright's guide to the Coast-to-Coast walk—a 192-mile footpath from the Irish Sea to the English Channel. To be fair, this book is probably not for everyone, as Wainwright is a bit dry. Wainwright, however, was about what you would expect from an English guy who spent most of his life walking around the English countryside; a disheveled recluse. He is not an explorer by any means, but rather a wanderer and is often described as "fell wanderer." Wainwright is full of good advice like, "There's no such thing as bad weather, only unsuitable clothing,"

and some inspiring stuff too, "You were made to soar, to crash to earth, then to rise and soar again."

In the spring of 2006, after driving my co-workers nuts for six months because I was working everyone to death, I convinced a friend to go on the Coast-to-Coast walk with me. We set out in the spring from St Bees on the Irish Sea and twelve days of walking and 192 miles later we arrived in Robin Hoods Bay on the other side of the country.

I do not know what it was about that experience that had a calming effect on me. What I learned as a leader is that sometimes you have to take things slow. In the three years I spent in the UK, I drove my car and took the train everywhere—I don't remember any of the details of driving or taking the train. I remember a million details of walking across England.

I can't explain why this veteran's reflections have touched me so deeply. Perhaps it's because I imagine that as someone whose career has been military, he had to deal with many instances of the unexpected. Yet he was open to a completely different form of being surprised and the wisdom it offered him. Perhaps it touches me because I too have been a driven leader and have found it hard to maintain a more human pace. Possibly it stays with me because I was so surprised by his unexpected thoughtfulness. Or, it could be because I overlooked his talents in our class, and I don't want to do that again, anytime, anywhere.

I think back to Max duPree, the Herman Miller CEO, who was delighted, then dismayed, to realize the beautiful poetry read at the millwright's wake had been written by the craftsman himself.

The Art and Spirit of Leadership
judybrown@aol.com   www.judysorumbrown.com

Millwright

He told the story
of the Millwright,
an hourly employee
in the trades,
who was,
as it turned out,
a poet,
and the leader
didn't know.
His is the story
of a sudden turning
of a corner
where we see
the gifts in someone else,
someone we thought we knew,
akin to sudden turning
of a corner
where we see the gifts
in us,
grieving that
it took so long.
Those turnings
are so tender.
Why are they then
so rare?

Judy Brown, March 22, 2002

The Art and Spirit of Leadership
judybrown@aol.com   www.judysorumbrown.com

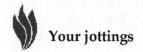 **Your jottings**

So often when we are looking in a certain direction or for a particular thing, we miss what is just off to the side, out of our direct line of sight. Or we have had hopes dashed by life and as a result are blind to the jewels that lie before us.

The Art and Spirit of Leadership
judybrown@aol.com www.judysorumbrown.com

Sometimes the gifts come out of seeming disappointments, expectations unmet. Puanani Burgess, a native Hawaiian community leader and gifted story-teller told a group of us about a time when she'd been asked to give an important speech to a large group—300 were expected. She spent much time preparing her thoughts, yet on arrival found only 30 people. The organizer of the event suggested that Puanani had not been as great a draw as anticipated, that it was her fault there wasn't a better turnout. Puanani did her best with the presentation, but arrived back home dispirited and disappointed.

Her 8-year old son, seeing her dejection, asked what had happened. After listening to her explanation, her son said, "I know there were only 30 people, but, Mom, what if one of them was Gandhi? What if one of them was me?"

Perhaps the great dancer Martha Graham was right in telling us not to judge our gifts, nor even to note how they are received, but just to keep the channel open, keep offering them to the world. And to create conditions where others, too, can surprise us with their gifts.

Often, for the fun of it, and for a change of pace, when I am exploring with executives this matter of being open to surprise, and to the gifts others bring us in dialogue, I invite them into a "gift exchange" exercise.

"Up on your feet," I say, "We're going to experiment with giving and receiving gifts."

"I need a volunteer to demonstrate this with me. Then in a minute, all of you are going to do what we do. First you pantomime giving your partner a surprise gift. In silence."

The Art and Spirit of Leadership
judybrown@aol.com   www.judysorumbrown.com

So, I pantomime giving the volunteer beside me a very heavy, awkward something. Then I begin a dialogue about that thing.

"I know it's heavy," I say, "and muddy and probably not well, but when I saw this old Golden Retriever in the ditch by the road, I thought if anyone could bring it back to health it would be you, because you are so kind."

My volunteer partner then has to join into the conversation about this "gift" she has received. No matter that she thought it was a glorious rose bush, the conversation is now about a muddy dog she is holding.

Then we demonstrate round two: I give her another gift, but this time, she gets to start the conversation. I think I have given her a handful of diamonds; she starts the conversation as if it were heritage tomato seeds. I have to forget about the diamonds I had in mind and join in a conversation about tomato seeds. Then we switch with her doing the gift-giving.

Once people have the idea, they begin to pantomime giving each other gifts. The room erupts into laughter. Someone thought she was getting a fur coat; it turned out to be a boa constrictor. Someone else thought she was being handed walnuts, and it turned out to be the keys to a new sports car. Light hearted. Playful. But a wonderful embodied reminder that the world is full of unexpected surprises, gifts, not all welcome at the moment.

The Art and Spirit of Leadership
judybrown@aol.com   www.judysorumbrown.com

And whether we admit it to ourselves or not, we always enter situations with expectations. Whether we are conscious of the expectations and assumptions, there they are—and must be set aside in order to see what is really being offered.

Being open to the unexpected is our only path to seeing the giftedness before us.

As my writing of these many pages has evolved over several months, it has been easy to fall into a sense of "assignment," of "task," of "to-do list," even of "deadlines" of my own making, rather than seeing the gifts in the very process of writing.

Yesterday, as the manuscript got larger and seemingly less manageable, I began to wonder what I could find to put it in, something that would be a practical "holder" for these words. I rummaged around the family cottage looking for boxes, but nothing was the right size. Then I came across a brightly colored gift bag, tucked away in a cupboard, neatly folded, flat. Left there, no doubt, by my mother, who died more than thirty years ago. The answer became a simple one: I put my writing, this book, chapter by chapter, in a decorative gift bag. Without even, at first, realizing the message I'd sent myself. This process of writing is a gift. So now, each morning as I grow closer to the concluding pages, I look with appreciation at the red and white gift bag that holds my words to travel, soon, to you.

How do we remember that our words, our writing, our story, are a gift? How do we live our lives with the belief that the people before us are gifted, miraculous? That the unexpected is a handful of diamonds? How to live as if Gandhi were in the group before us or part of our team? Or that a beloved child is among those learning with us?

How would that change our reaction to the unexpected, the surprise? And what would we then think possible, among us, even a small group of us?

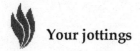 **Your jottings**

Gifts II

The day brings
its own gifts.
I might have wanted
something else,
or worried
that another thing
would happen.
But it all unfolds
in its own way—
the day does—
naturally,
being itself.
It brings
these gifts
quite unanticipated.

Judy Brown, November 3, 2005

Chapter Eight

Take The Risk Of Being Less Than Perfect

A recent poem of mine, "I wish I'd bought my father cashmere socks" reminds me how often we feel we are not generous enough, patient enough, thoughtful enough. You can fill in the words that rattle around in your own mind. And yet, none of us is perfect. No matter where we are in life.

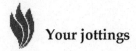 **Your jottings**

I wish I'd bought my father cashmere socks

I wish
I'd bought
my father
cashmere socks.
His feet
were gnarled,
his skin
was sensitive.
In months
he would be gone.
He needed socks.
I stopped
somewhere
inconsequential
and got socks that were OK—
the first pair
I could find.
A little rough.
But strong.
They'd last.

Almost two decades
have now passed.
It's just
a small regret,
yet lingering.
I wish
I'd bought
my father
cashmere socks.

Judy Brown, April 1, 2011

 The Art and Spirit of Leadership
judybrown@aol.com   www.judysorumbrown.com

And, for those of us in leadership roles, perhaps we are most prone to try to achieve perfection, or pretend we have it, or are at least modeling it. There seems to be something terrifying for many of us in admitting our own imperfections—small or large. To realize we have made mistakes. To concede we can't figure it out alone, that we can't do it alone. Admitting we need help. Even uttering the phrase, "I don't know" can be tough. And still, it is in holding that human, imperfect and unknowing space, where we invite the participation and gifts of others, that we are most open to being alive, to stretching ourselves.

Yet so often, when we feel lost or uncertain, we keep our own counsel until we are sure we know, until we have it perfect, at least perfect enough, for us to let the world see the results of our effort. A colleague e-mailed me recently:

> A woman I love recently died—had been ill, but with incredible spirit, style and true *elan*, a full beating heart, bright eyes, raucous laugh, red wine in hand—and I wanted to pass along one thing from the gathering we had after she left us.

> She had been in recent conversation with a smart, open-minded female Methodist pastor about all things existential and she gave one of her coolest wall hangings to this pastor, which says "Begin anywhere" and which the pastor shared with the gathering. Calm but fierce. A challenge and a meditation.

Begin anywhere, indeed.

I have disciplined myself never to second-guess messages that come to me in such a fashion, or conversations that begin, "Somehow I thought you should know about this." This was the case of my colleague describing her father's refusal to move off the packing box he was sitting on. Or strangers who come up and

The Art and Spirit of Leadership
judybrown@aol.com www.judysorumbrown.com

say, "Everything's connected. Everything's changing. So pay attention." Or words of wisdom from the taxi driver Leon when he says, "It doesn't have to be perfect to be good."

Deepak Chopra, in his book, *The Spontaneous Fulfillment of Desire*, notes the remarkable way that ideas and people and images are connected just below the surface of things in ways that our logical minds and our focused eyes can miss. This web of connection can be an enormous support in times when we are less than perfect, and life is making challenging demands on us where the response is not clear.

"Begin anywhere."

The public policy variant on this life lesson of "Begin Anywhere" is evident in a recent *Washington Post* headline: "The Motor City mayor's engine for change; desperate and depopulated, Detroit offers itself up as a lab for experimentation." This is a front page story of a leader who is saying, "It is worse than I thought; I don't know the path forward. Come help us." The article goes on to speak of an artist, community leader and entrepreneur who, with great spirit and hope, responded, "It's open season." Open season on good creative, innovative ideas because a leader is willing to stand up and say, "I need help."

"Begin Anywhere." Yet I realize how naïve such an idea can sound. And even how dangerous, as we think about the unexpected, unintended consequences of what might seem to be great ideas at the time. But if we are alive to the world around us, we must engage with it. Thoughtfully.

I often encourage leaders to think of the practices of leadership as if they were scientists undertaking experiments about what works. We need an experimental mind-set in learning and leading. We need a willingness to move forward even if the path isn't perfect.

The Art and Spirit of Leadership
judybrown@aol.com   www.judysorumbrown.com

Experiments

You have to have
experiments to evaluate—
someone of courage
or obsession,
or deeper knowing,
throwing caution
or large sums of money
to the winds,
says simply,
"We're going to do this
just because it's right.
I know it's hard.
It's right."
And later, on reflection,
folks will say,
"It isn't perfect.
There are problems."

Small snakes in Eden,
I suppose.
But Eden wouldn't be there
to evaluate
had some prophetic
human being never said,
"We're doing it
because it's right."

Judy Brown, August 7, 2007

The Art and Spirit of Leadership
judybrown@aol.com www.judysorumbrown.com

One of my greatest guides in this idea of willingness to experiment, to put pen to paper and ideas into practice, is William Stafford, poet laureate of Oregon. He, as I mentioned earlier, encouraged Minnesota poet Robert Bly to take up the practice of writing "morning poems"–and not worry so much about the quality as the practice of writing.

The conversation between these two poets concerns much more than writing poems. It reminds me that if I wait for perfection, I'll never get going. I'll never put words on paper to see how they look. I'll never play the piano because the piece I am practicing won't sound great the first time I sit down with it. I won't try kayaking because, as I said to a friend, "I look like a walrus trying to get out of a soap-dish." But then I'll never get to float in the back channels of our creek under the trees on a dreamy summer morning.

The idea that excellence stems from "lowering our standards" is a counter-intuitive notion. Thurber admonishes us: "Don't get it right, just get it written." Recognizing that insistence on our own perfection can keep us stuck is an important awareness. For those who lead and those who wish to continue to learn.

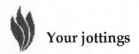 **Your jottings**

Perfection fails us

Perfection
fails us,
breaks down,
eventually,
disintegrates.
It's being human
that can save us
from the clutches
of the fearful
unexpected.
It's letting
ourselves
feel what's true,
riding the waves
of joy or pain,
like some tsunami
where we are safer
far from shore,
and time
will bring us
home again.

Judy Brown, January 5, 2005

The Art and Spirit of Leadership
judybrown@aol.com   www.judysorumbrown.com

The courage to offer thoughts still "a-greening," ideas that may be (especially in the emotional dimension) "raggedy," as my friend Geno Schnell calls them, opens the path to new possibilities and new understanding. Letting go of the driving necessity for perfection, forgiving ourselves our imperfections, allows us to need others, to rely on others. We invite others into the game with us. Because we are not "perfect," but are human, we invite community, connection and collective action.

Some of my most memorable experiences of this dynamic have come from instances where I simply have had to throw myself on the mercy of my colleagues or (even worse) my clients: Years back I flew out to California to lead a weekend retreat for a group of dispirited hospital nurses, still reeling from the shock of huge earthquakes and hospital reorganizations. They were living with the cracks, literal and figurative, in their hospital, and they were still unsteady from that experience. We gathered at a mountaintop resort, to step away from all that danger and anxiety. And as luck would have it, we had an earthquake up there—my first ever experience of looking out at a neatly mown lawn and seeing it begin to move in soft waves like Lake Michigan does when the wind comes up. Unnerving!

And if that weren't bad enough, I, the leader of this retreat, had developed an arresting case of laryngitis. I could not speak. So all I could do was listen and then post a question on the easel for the group to wrestle with. Thankfully, the laryngitis had not ruined my skill with magic markers.

So for an entire weekend, I was silent. And they spoke with each other. They found the retreat remarkably helpful, healing, and fun. I found it a revelation. My greatest value to the nurses did not lie in being perfect, and certainly not in having all the answers, but in simply listening carefully and posing good questions to keep their answers flowing. And then listening some more.

It's hard as leaders, as teachers, to hold onto the idea that our contributions may arise as much from our imperfections, our human vulnerabilities, as from our strengths. So the universe thumped me with two resounding refresher lessons this year to remind me of the truth that first came to me on the mountaintop with the nurses, when I could not speak—and everyone liked how things went.

This year I pulled a back muscle a few days before I was scheduled to drive to Cleveland with two young colleagues to lead a program for leaders in aging services. Suddenly I became a statue. Frozen. I could barely walk. I went to the doctor. He said it wasn't dire, but I should rest and lie on my back (not sit) on the couch with knees bent. For several days.

"But," I said, "I have to go to Cleveland." "Well," he replied, "the only thing worse than an airplane seat in these circumstances is a car. And in case you were figuring on riding lying down on the back seat, that's the worst of all." That actually was what I had in mind. I went home figuring over the weekend I'd have a miraculous recovery. But, by Saturday it was evident that no miracle was going to be forthcoming.

So I was forced to call my two colleagues, feeling abject and totally useless, and tell them I was benched. They were gracious and understanding, told me to take care of myself and drove off to Cleveland on their own. I lay on my back that week, trying to remind myself that these two smart, talented colleagues would handle things just fine without me. Although I wasn't sure if the best news would be that they had (and therefore I was unnecessary) or that they hadn't (and it was through my failings that things had gone badly.)

What actually happened was a third scenario that had never occurred to me: Things went really well, they felt increasingly confident about their skills, and they and everyone else really

219   The Art and Spirit of Leadership

missed me. They asked if it would be OK if they extended my contract with them from one year to three and gave me a raise. I was stunned. My head is still reeling.

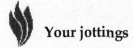 **Your jottings**

Relay

I thought
it was a marathon,
the work
that must be done.
I learned
it was a relay.
That changed everything.

Judy Brown, November 27, 2008

The Art and Spirit of Leadership
judybrown@aol.com www.judysorumbrown.com

The final blow to my stubborn idea of the importance of perfection, invincibility and invulnerability and always leading things came this fall. My graduate leadership class began, as in the story about Caroline White, with the reminder that "We meet for seven all-day Friday sessions, so it's imperative we are all present for all the sessions." On our fifth Friday together, I awoke at 5 a.m. feeling terrible. It felt like the flu. It was the Friday before Thanksgiving week and the last thing I wanted to do was expose 21 people to something they would then carry across the country to friends and family at Thanksgiving. So I did the only thing I could think of. I sent the following e-mail, took a deep breath went back to bed and hoped for the best:

> On Fri, Nov 19, 2010 at 6:39 AM,
> <JudyBrown@aol.com> wrote:
>
> Dear One and All,
>
> Since last we met I've been thinking of how often good leadership is a collective effort. Someone asks a particularly good question, someone else suggests a path forward. And it looks like we'll get to practice the collective nature of our work together today. I seem to have picked up some kind of stomach bug that I don't want to share with you. And so I am going to stay home and invite you all to guide each other through today's work.
>
> Here's a suggestion for a path, although you may decide on another one for the day.
>
> Our goal is to soak up as much as we can about each others' second texts—particularly as they might represent, certain of them, a resource to our thinking about the understanding (framing) of leadership we want to carry forward in our own lives. And that is, of

course, the subject for the final papers. But more than that, it is an important matter for each of us as we move forward in our lives.

Today is a day to really get our arms around that body of knowledge.

Here's a suggestion of a plan:

Check-in What I'd want you to know about my life these days…and what I am increasingly noticing about leadership…(if someone is willing to take notes and share them with me, I'd appreciate that).

Second text presentations—those that remain, plus any additional insights from those who went early and now, thinking about the second text paper, have more to say to us. One of you might want to guide that process, making sure there is space for questions and conversation after each paper, and that there is enough time to hear about all the second texts.

Then I'd suggest you break into teams of 4, then one at a time and then in conversation, explore for each of you which of the other texts are currently standing out as an important resource to you, and why. Upon returning to the full group, you might see if there are particular threads of that conversation that bear sharing with the entire class.

If time remains, anyone who is ready to share the insights of their leadership shadow might do that (again, I'd love to have notes on that so I have a sense of the insights).

The Art and Spirit of Leadership
judybrown@aol.com   www.judysorumbrown.com

Then a check-out: wishes for Thanksgiving, perhaps. Whatever is on your mind.

I will be at home and near a phone, if you need to call me for any reason. But I expect you will do splendidly with your own collective guidance and wisdom. I look forward to hearing how things have gone. One or another (or many) of you, be sure and fill me in.

Take good care,
Judy

There were no calls. Instead, there were e-mails after class with news of wonderful developments. The first student e-mail came from a very seasoned Department of Defense executive and former staffer on Capitol Hill:

You will probably receive a few emails on this but class went very well today. You have done a great job of inspiring the class to work their way through these issues. There was never really a need to move the class along as everything flowed and probably the only risk we faced was over-staying our time talking through issues on a Holiday weekend. That was the only intervention I thought I had to make was to plan out our time at the end so we didn't go too long as our agenda was looking too ambitious for the time remaining. This couldn't have happened in the first couple of weeks of class. It was really quite amazing. I was quite impressed by the events of the day.

And this from another mid-career student:

By the way, I'm sure you've already heard this from others, but the class on Friday was amazing. I've never been part of a class that would go on for the entire time, with full participation from everyone, in the absence of the professor. What a testament to the environment you've established, and to the way the class has bonded as a community.

It has taken three very formative experiences for me to realize it is our vulnerability, our imperfections even, that allows people to connect to us. That allows them, even invites them, to step in and join the collaborative work of leadership. And that it may open up a new and more fruitful dynamic among us.

I think again and again of my friend Dee's question: "When do you feel fragile?" Not "Do you feel fragile?" but "When do you feel fragile?" My questions for myself, now: "What is possible when we operate openly and authentically from that place of fragile humanity? How much more alive might we be?"

It was a group of little children, however, who taught me the most lasting lesson about the power of lightening up on perfection— and propriety. When my husband and I were dating, I would, from time to time, visit him where he lived and worked on the island of Providenciales in the Turks and Caicos Islands. He had a network of friends there and somehow, the word got out that his girlfriend was a poet.

The first-grade daughter of one friend was also a poet and wanted to bring a grown-up poet to "show and tell" at school—and so I found myself sitting in a rocker, feeling a bit like a gerbil or pet mouse on display, with a circle of young poets sitting on the floor around me. They were talking about writing, asking me questions and they asked me to read one of my poems. "Which one would you like?" I asked. A hand shot up. "The one about no underwear." I was completely thrown. How in the world did the first graders get their hands on that one, and why did it intrigue them?

The Art and Spirit of Leadership
judybrown@aol.com www.judysorumbrown.com

But they had asked and I felt duty bound to honor their request. I would read the poem "Permission" — what they termed the "no underwear poem." It was an admission of the life-giving power of giving ourselves permission to be imperfect and to be human.

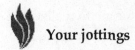 **Your jottings**

The Art and Spirit of Leadership
judybrown@aol.com www.judysorumbrown.com

Permission

I tell myself —
As I move
slowly
down the
front walk
of my house
underneath the
oaks,
starting on my
morning walk —
I tell myself
that
I can
walk
as long
as I want,
as slow
as I want,
without
a watch,
and without
a bra or panties
underneath
my cotton shirt
and jeans,
and only sandals
on my feet,

The Art and Spirit of Leadership
judybrown@aol.com   www.judysorumbrown.com

and no place
in particular
to go.
Moving
like
a slow boat
on sea swells,
or a
Conestoga wagon
crossing
the windswept prairie
slowly,
moving
like a cathedral-bound
processional of one,
I notice
the scent
of blooming
trees
whose flowers
are breathing
out their
odor in the
summer sun,
the touch
against my ankles
of the uncut
grass in the field
just beyond the woods,
and the scent
of a handsome
man who smiling
passes by me
on the sidewalk

underneath the
trees along
the stream,
and the softness
of my jeans
against my thighs,
and the
pale half-moon
half hidden
in the blue
mid-morning sky,
and the Japanese
dogwood in bloom,
and the late white azaleas
which have no scent,
and the distant indistinct
chatter of other walkers
hidden by the trees,
and the panting
of a huge yellow dog
running beside his owner,
and a black-bird
flying straight through
the trees at eye-level
with food in her mouth.
At this pace
everything's
alive. And so
am I.

Judy Brown, June 1, 2002

The Art and Spirit of Leadership
judybrown@aol.com   www.judysorumbrown.com

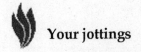 **Your jottings**

Chapter Nine

Lead With Story and Invite Stories From Others

Sharing real and heartfelt stories from our lives helps people know who we are. Stories create natural, memorable and lasting bonds among people, even people whose backgrounds and experiences seem wildly different.

When leaders offer stories about what has shaped their lives and their outlook, it creates space for insights on the part of their team. It builds a sense of trust that comes from knowing who someone is "through and through."

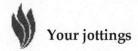 **Your jottings**

Stories

Why do we need
to hear
the stories,
tell our own?
Perhaps our DNA,
our tribe,
creates within a hunger
for the pattern
of the sounds.
Most of us
grew up in a story
we call family—
the isolated notion
of one moment
congregates
around a story theme
like fudge still cooking
congregates around a spoon.

Our moments stick to one another
like fine grains of sand
collecting into something larger,
larger still,
until the story carries us,
creates a path on which we journey,
and traveling that way,
mysteriously
the story tells us
what we've longed
to know.

Judy Brown, November 15, 2006

The Art and Spirit of Leadership
judybrown@aol.com   www.judysorumbrown.com

Humans hunger for story. And one can lead with story in a variety of ways. The very use of the word "story" in organizational life creates a richer understanding of the complexity and the dynamics that surround our work together. It helps us become conscious of the way organizations are woven of the threads of many stories.

We can talk about the story of our organization, of the stories we tell ourselves about our current circumstances, of the future story we wish to tell about ourselves and the story that might be told about how we achieved that future. This helps us keep in mind that when we say "the reality is" or "the truth is," we have forgotten that generally "reality" and "truth" are the bottom line of some story we tell ourselves.

When people come together from "two different sides," sharing stories can erase the gulf which they think divides them. A colleague, newly elected as County Executive of one of our most diverse and dynamic counties, was bringing together his team— half hold-overs from the prior administration and half new players. In their first staff retreat, he wondered how we might help them see one another as colleagues and as allies.

> We asked everyone in the room, all 80 of the leaders, to take notes on their own story—the stepping stones that had brought them to where they were in their work and their life. And also to sketch what they saw as the story of the county—the stepping stones, the major events that had shaped the county.
>
> Then on a long wall, I stretched a sixty-foot long sheet of butcher-block paper, a long, long expanse of it, with the decades marked off beginning around 1900, well before those in the room were born, and carrying through to the current year. I asked everyone to mark on that long timeline the milestones of his own life and family (parents

The Art and Spirit of Leadership
judybrown@aol.com   www.judysorumbrown.com

immigrated from Poland, first child born, elected to county council), as well as those of the county as they knew them.

When their work was done, the threads of immigration of their parents, of their grandparents, and of some of the leaders themselves, were evident. The births and the deaths that had marked their lives. And the roles in which they had served and from which they had learned.

When people finished making their notations on the long scroll on the wall, they stood back, captivated, and read the notes from others.

Our conversation then was about the patterns that stood out: immigration, achievement, struggle, resilience, the power of community. The conversation itself wove us together into a single leadership group.

Then I asked the county executive, a modest, quiet man of remarkable achievement, to talk about what in his own life had brought him to where he was. He spoke about growing up as a sharecropper in the South, his mother's strength and determination, his military service—words spoken in a room totally silent, as people listened—words that created an indelible sense of the human being leading them and a respect for the humanness of all.

On another occasion, working with the city administrator of one of our large communities, I suggested a similar process: individuals would jot down the stepping stones that had brought them to where they were in their work and their life. Then folks would share them in trios, with a conversation to follow in the full group.

The city administrator thought such a process was unnecessary, as they had worked together for some time and as she said, "We know each other well." "Humor me," I said. So they did.

As they shared their life stepping stones in the groups of three, they were astonished to realize that they had rich threads of history in common they hadn't known about—family histories of military service, childhoods shaped by parents who took one service assignment after another, moving their families. They had important formative experiences and capacities unknown to one another, almost unknown to themselves. Like many of us, in the compelling desire to serve, we forget the stories that brought us to that service.

Telling their stories revealed surprises, unexpected links, and a much deeper understanding of the richness that they represented to each other. Knowing that created new and stronger bonds. And it was fun, heart-warming.

In work that my colleague Michael Jones and I do with executives, we invite people into "story cafés" – tables of four with round-robin story-telling focused on one of a variety of themes. Sometimes it is stories of a time of courage in their lives. Another time it might be stories of a time of facing into something unwelcome and years later being proud of how they handled it. Sometimes stories of an unexpected surprise. Or stories of a place that has a special meaning and how it came to have that meaning for them.

Whatever the question, the format is always the same: First a few moments of silence as people take notes in their journals about the story that comes to mind. Then one at a time, with 15 minutes for each person, people tell their story and their three colleagues just listen, wholeheartedly, without comment, soaking up the story.

Leading with story carries a subtle and important message: the speaker is the sole authority on what they say, on the story they tell about their life. And on the meaning they give to it.

This practice helps people grasp the importance of respecting the perspective of the other, even when that perspective differs from their own. And it helps us remember that in almost any circumstance, there will be a variety of perspectives that differ from one another, subtly or vividly, and that are critical to a full understanding of the situation.

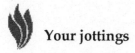 **Your jottings**

It also says that you remain the sole "author" of the story of your life; in that role you have no possible competitor.

The Art and Spirit of Leadership
judybrown@aol.com www.judysorumbrown.com

Competitor

You have
no possible
competitor
in being
wholly who you are.
In such
a race
as that,
the field
is completely
yours.

Judy Brown, June 19, 2004

When people know our story, they are more likely to be drawn to join us in an effort. And, in knowing one another's stories, they are more likely to feel connected to each other in the effort.

So one of our roles as a leader is to invite story out of others. The authentic, the whole, the heartfelt. The stories of places from which we have come. Stories of people who have drawn out our best efforts. Stories of mistakes. Stories of successes. Stories of surprises.

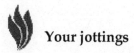 **Your jottings**

Stories II

When the stories
begin and we listen,
really listen
to each other,
we begin
to notice
that we are not
quite so much the same
as we had thought,
at least
not in the ways
we thought.
And we are not
so different as we thought,
at least not in the ways
we thought.
And like some
big old family
full of odd relatives,
we are all kin,
befuddled
and beloved.

Judy Brown, July 3, 2005

The Art and Spirit of Leadership
judybrown@aol.com   www.judysorumbrown.com

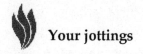 **Your jottings**

The Art and Spirit of Leadership
judybrown@aol.com   www.judysorumbrown.com

Sometimes the important story is the story of why we think the way we do. But it's not easy to get people to surface openly what they think and why they think it. As I mentioned, the idea "I think therefore I am," has led us to believe that our thoughts are our selves, and therefore to share them openly leaves us open to attack. Any attack on our thinking, our ideas, feels like an attack on our essence, on "who I am." To have our ideas or thought process challenged is to be personally attacked.

So even speaking thoughts clearly and openly can be a risk, or at least feel like a risk. But if we aren't able to share our thoughts and ideas, we risk even more. We risk not hearing a perspective or an insight from one among us who can help us solve some problem or avert a disaster. When story-telling occurs and is respected, we create spaces for the kind of real speaking and real listening that leads to productive sharing of ideas instead of debates or personal attacks. We are able, as Susan Scott says, to "Get out from behind ourselves."

Too often, however, we hide our thinking from one another, not wanting to rock the boat or to expose our assumptions. Creating conditions where real speaking and real listening become natural is not easy. It seems to occur most easily and naturally where the format is story—where story-telling occurs and is respected— since it is the very tone of story that keeps us from falling into debates or arguments.

Recently in my graduate public policy leadership course, one of the students said "We should have a dialogue about how people feel we are doing as a country." Total silence followed that suggestion. We had just lived through one of those painful weeks where events seemed to have taken a disheartening downturn, nationally and internationally.

Startled, I wondered how to create a respectful and constructive learning conversation, rather than an argument or debate, among twenty-one gifted, diverse people who spanned generations, came from cultures around the world, and had served as visible public leaders, private sector managers, and likely undercover agents. What popped into my mind was a process I'd read about the day before, described by a leader in Authentic Leadership in Action (formerly known as the Shambhala Institute). In a moment of high creativity (or brash risk-taking, perhaps), I decided to try that practice and see its impact on the quality of our conversation.

"OK," I said. "We're going to take this conversation out of this classroom and into the atrium. I want you to imagine that the end of the atrium by the ladies room represents this position: 'I think the whole situation is hopeless and a mess.' And the other end of the atrium by the computer lab stands for 'I actually think there are signs of hope in all this.'"

"I want you to put yourself on that continuum between despair and possibility by standing on the spot that best represents your current thinking about how we are doing as a country."

We all scrambled out of the room into the school's public space. Folks jostled about until they felt they were in the right spot. "OK, now," I said. "We're going to hear from individuals about why they are standing where they are standing. Tell us the story behind how you came to be where you are. And if what you hear from someone moves you to change your position, just do so. Let's see what we learn. Who wants to go first?"

One of the folks way down by the ladies room spoke first, detailing what he was seeing and why he was so dispirited by it. People listened. A couple of people moved a little more in his direction. Then someone down by the computer lab said, "I actually see the same indicators, but I

243   The Art and Spirit of Leadership

think they are hopeful signs. We're finally admitting what is really going on, and that will prompt much more open dialogue across the usual divisions in the country." One person moved a couple of steps in her direction.

We continued that way for half an hour or so. One at a time, someone would talk, and then some people would move. Or not. Then we went back into our classroom. I asked people what struck them.

One thoughtful student said, "It was so helpful to be able to just think about where I wanted to stand, and why, and simply stand there. Not having to figure out what was going on with other people—because I could see where they were without having to try to guess about it."

As people laid out the story of why they were standing where they were standing in the public center of the public policy school, there emerged among us a much deeper understanding of the thoughts and the experiences behind our positions. And no one seemed even tempted to argue with anyone else about where they were. It was simply their spot, and what they had to say was their story of why they chose that spot.

My friend Mary Parish and I teach a course on "The Leadership Power of Story," and we often work with groups much more drawn to power point and the bottom line than story. We remind them, laughing, that we are all part of the same species that grew up on the savannah, around the fire at night, telling stories about the day's hunt.

And we remind them that story "sticks." It is much more memorable than even the most compelling data. There is something generous about story, something that feels more like an offering, a gift, than a sales pitch. Something that allows it to travel like stealth technology, by-passing our usual judgment and resistance. Moving from "I don't think so" and inviting us to "consider this."

 Your jottings

Bone deep

How can we return
to what we know
bone deep?
And share it?
Not as some stern advice,
but as a gift,
a bit of sweet,
some of our story,
something that's rich,
that we would
want the other
to enjoy.

Judy Brown, March 20, 2011

Chapter Ten

Follow The Threads Of Aliveness

I frequently find myself recalling William Stafford's words in his poem "The way it is" about the thread we follow in life, each life different and each thread different, yet consistent throughout each of our lives. He reminds me that we must pay attention to the thread, the path of aliveness, of being, in our own lives. And we need to be sensitive to the threads of aliveness in the lives of others.

It is far too easy to lose sight of what has real life for us. What the woodcarver calls a "live encounter." Once at a particularly tough time in my life, when I found my attention being continually drawn to what wasn't working, to things that were deadening to me, I pulled out a sheet of paper and wrote at the top "People who draw my best energies." I had no idea what I meant by those words. But I set about peppering the paper with the names of people whose very existence brought forth my spirit, my best efforts—colleagues, friends, even writers I did not know, but whose words perked me up.

Thinking to myself, "Well what was that all about?" I folded the paper and tucked it into my journal. Three months later a piece of folded paper fell out of the journal. I picked it up and opened it. It took me a moment to recognize it. It was the paper with twenty-two names of people who "brought out my best energies," who represented a "live encounter" for me. Even reading their names made my heart sing.

Then, I realized something really startling: in those three months I had been in touch with or working with all twenty-two of them! I couldn't tell you how it had happened. To this day, I wonder at it. Over that period of three months, something had directed my

The Art and Spirit of Leadership
judybrown@aol.com www.judysorumbrown.com

attention away from all that was deadening and towards positive sources of life. My energies followed my attention. And my life was dramatically different.

Sometimes the thread of aliveness is emotional and raggedy. You know things are "alive" because there is high emotion of one kind or another. I think back to a memorable experience with a group of teachers in a series of retreats we led over a period of two years. My co-facilitator and I had chosen an elegant country retreat site with fine cuisine. But our participants, urban public school teachers, were not as fond as we were of rare roast beef and some of the more exotic foods and styles of preparation. Mealtime was jarring to them, far from what they considered welcoming, homelike. So they got just plain hungry when we gathered. And hungry people get grumpy.

By the time we gathered for our second retreat, the dissatisfaction with the place and its fancy food, erupted into wide-spread collective unhappiness. My colleague, whose own values held that generosity meant elegant, beautiful food, felt personally attacked. She was as caught up in the dynamic as our teachers.

Because our norm in the retreats was to "listen each other into our own truth," I gathered us in a dialogue that we later called the "food fight." I kept reminding myself that I didn't have to understand what was going on, or agree with it; I just needed to stay with the thread of it. Stafford's words, "… you don't ever let go of the thread" were ringing in my ears. I just held on. I kept repeating to myself that it was OK to be surprised. I just had to follow the thread of the conversation, to be witness to, and appreciative of, the challenges here for myself and for others.

I found myself repeatedly asking, when there was a lull in the conversation, "Is there more?" And there was. For a full two hours there was more. And after that, things settled down. With our newly gained insights, my colleague and I were able to adjust the menu and other aspects of our work together that were frustrating our teachers, and we were able to resume our collective work.

Perhaps more importantly, we all understood that we could talk openly about real frustrations and be heard. By following the thread of aliveness (frustration and dissatisfaction, in this case) among us and bearing witness to one another's frustrations, we came to a natural place of peaceful unity and settled back in together.

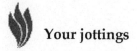 **Your jottings**

Sometimes the thread of aliveness is a life-time commitment to social action. A consistent "yes" to tackling the challenges of the world. Esther Webb's life represents that to me. An elder in our community at 90, she was still demonstrating for the causes she cared for—sometimes in a wheel chair, but always present.

judybrown@aol.com   www.judysorumbrown.com

Radical in Red (for Esther Webb)

She's our
radical in red,
now ninety,
standing beside
the birthday cake,
full of glee
at all the fuss.
Ever hopeful and determined,
in her red felt hat,
and big down scarlet parka-coat,
warm, bundled up,
she remains
joyful and determined,
her shoulder to the wheel of change
in every season.

Judy Brown, November 25, 2007

Sometimes the energy, the thread of aliveness is a resounding "NO." Roger Saillant tells the story about the Army Corps of Engineers' decision to create a cement channel for Detroit's River Rouge way upstream, near Roger's garden in Dearborn. Roger realized that the cementing of the natural stream would ruin his garden, among other things, and he was determined to stop the plan. Not withstanding the likelihood that his opposition to the Army Corps would bring him into conflict with his superiors at Ford, he was unrelenting in his "no" to that plan. His pursuit of that "no" through various networks of his own and through the courts, began a series of changes of direction in the city of Dearborn and likely at Ford.

I like to think that Roger's persistent "no" eventually contributed to the protection of the watershed and the now world-famous green redesign of Ford's original River Rouge Plant, which stands at the mouth of the river in downtown Detroit. Roger would no doubt demur about his influence, but sometimes turning points are marked by an individual powerful "no."

Why is the "no" so important?

My friend Marcial Losada has done research to trace communication dynamics of teams that get outstanding results. The pattern of communication he discerns suggests that the give and take of teams that "make it" is marked by six-to-one positivity or possibility thinking, as opposed to "limits setting." Or, as I would call it, the strong 'No. Six-to-one, possibilities to limits.

The surprise for me has been that what is essential to a positive effort is the power of the authentic "no." Not a rigid "no" or an unthinking "no," but rather "no" as guidance about limits, about necessary boundaries. About a perspective that needs be taken into account. As the peace-maker, the one who favors possibilities over limits, I have taken Marcial's research as an essential guide in my leadership.

The Art and Spirit of Leadership
judybrown@aol.com www.judysorumbrown.com

One of my favorite examples of the value of "no" comes from a powerful documentary called *Divided Highways* about the growth of the US interstate highway system. The documentary traces how Dwight Eisenhower, after seeing the German autobahn at the end of World War II, realized the importance of a broad network of highways for national defense. He became committed to building the US interstate system.

Divided Highways documents how the drive for national defense created a highway system that was the envy of the world. But that same drive created a runaway system that carved through family farms and poor urban communities, without any limits.

What began to put the brakes on it, was an unlikely "no." An older woman in a low-income Boston community was approached one day by two highway engineers who had been sent to tell her that she had to leave her house because the government was coming through with the highway. "What do you mean, the government is coming through?" she asked. "We are the government." And with those words, she bit the engineer. On his arm.

"She didn't bite me all that hard," the engineer said later.

Then he added with a tone of wistful puzzlement: "They just send us out to tell people the highway is coming and their house is in the way. I guess if someone came to my house and said I had to leave, I'd be upset, too." It was the absolute, heartfelt, authentic "no" represented by the lady biting the engineer that began to change the direction and the process of the highway expansion program.

Sometimes the "no" comes as a realization that what was once OK is no longer acceptable. Perhaps what once was seen a worthwhile effort, the building of the highways, has gone too far or veered too far off track and thus must now be faced with a "no."

I love the words from the Quaker hymnal describing a conversation between William Penn, the Quaker philosopher and political leader who founded Pennsylvania, and George Fox, the spiritual leader of the Society of Friends (Quakers), a sect opposed to all forms of violence:

> Will Penn said to George Fox, 'Oh what should I do?
> Can I wear this sword while I serve my God too?'
> George Fox said to Will Penn,
> You'll know when you're through.
> Just wear it, use it, but don't you abuse it.
> Just wear it as long as you can."

"Just wear it as long as you can." What a great piece of advice to all of us! This attunement to what is emerging as a "soft no" is a critical practice for knowing what makes our heart "sink" rather than sing. For knowing what is no longer "alive" for us. For knowing what we can't wear any longer.

And sometimes it is a hard "no." The "no" that means (in a tone much like my Mother's mid-western voice), "This will not do!" Such energy may create, in a charged moment, a framing of an alternative way of thinking, a framing that can change the dynamic.

I had such an experience years back when I was working with a gifted corporate and non-profit team exploring the sources of employee engagement. Our question: What were the leadership approaches that create a culture of engagement for people? It was wonderful spirited work, but some days our greatest challenge was our leader. Brilliant, but a bit erratic, he would now and again get caught up in his own anxieties and, just at the point that the work was most productive,

253   The Art and Spirit of Leadership

he would unleash all his fears on us as a team and we would go into a tailspin. It was a wild and unproductive dynamic.

I knew that we had somehow to break the pattern, but I didn't have a clue how. On the heels of one of these tail-spin disruptions, I found myself in a kind of flow state, furiously writing a list of five things on a piece of paper. This is what was on the paper.

Touchstones: Ideas that increase the likelihood of our working together productively

1) **Come to the work with 100% of the self.** Set aside the usual distractions of phone mail, e-mail, things undone from yesterday, things to do tomorrow. Bring all of yourself to the work, not just the parts of yourself and your experience that are obviously relevant to this work. Be 100% present here.

2) **Let the beauty we love be what we do.** Think of all the things you value and enjoy in life. Bring them with you in your peripheral vision. Bring their richness along as resources. Consider what they have to teach us about the dilemmas we are exploring today. Rumi says it best:

> Today, like every other day, we wake up empty and frightened. Don't open the door to the study and begin reading. Take down a musical instrument.

> Let the beauty we love be what we do.
> There are hundreds of ways to kneel and kiss the ground.

The Art and Spirit of Leadership
judybrown@aol.com www.judysorumbrown.com

3) **Presume welcome and extend welcome.** We all learn most effectively in spaces which welcome us. Therefore, welcome each other to this place and this work and presume that we are welcome in turn.

4) **Nose into inquiry.** When we feel challenged or confused, switch from saying to asking, from advocating to inquiring, from knowing to wondering, from stating to questioning. Like a canoe trying to make headway into the wind, nose straight into the wind, head into inquiry. When it's hard, turn to wonder.

5) **Consider that it is possible to emerge from the conversation refreshed, wondering, curious, surprised.** Expect that our time together will provide for renewal, refreshment, helpful perspectives on the work at hand. Our work is not about more "to-do", but rather about more effortless ways to do that which we must do.

Those five items, shared as they came out of my pen that day, turned us around. And over the years they have provided helpful guidance for staying on track (and out of the ditch) to many groups with which I have collaborated. They have functioned as a centerpiece of the Courage and Renewal work with Parker Palmer and our colleagues. Yet only now do I realize the full extent to which they came out of the energy of the hard "no," the realization that "this won't do."

I think what surprised me then and continues to surprise me now is the wisdom that can emerge from following the threads of our frustration with a difficult dynamic. I continue to learn how that thread of frustration, when listened to and creatively incorporated, can provide guidance toward an alternative path.

For me, creative processes, poetry, even this kind of design that emerged out of despair, has that mark of guidance from beyond myself. Guidance that is whole and complete. Seemingly dashed out on a slip of paper. Done. I think many of us have that same capacity for listening to inner wisdom. It arises from the unstoppable force of energy when some part of us realizes that this behavior "will not do!" I recall a story about Jesse Jackson from years back that has always helped me understand that kind of energy and its power:

> As the story goes, some group had captured an American and was holding him in a prison in Jerusalem. Jesse Jackson, hearing of this at a meeting in Chicago, decided in one moment that this situation was not acceptable. Not OK! And he (believe me, this was not in his job description) took immediate action.

> He walked out of the Chicago hotel, hailed a cab, and said "Take me to Jerusalem." The cabbie looked at him, and said, "Well, Buddy, I can get you as far as O'Hare." And he did. Jackson got out of the cab at O'Hare Airport, and said to the baggage handler at the curb, "I want to go to Jerusalem," and the guy responded, "Well I'd check with Tel Aviv Airways, if I were you, upstairs."

> Jackson went up the stairs and said to the agent at the Tel Aviv counter, "Take me to Jerusalem." The man said, "Well, we can get you as far as Tel Aviv." And he sold Jackson a ticket for the next flight. When Jackson got off the flight in Tel Aviv, he hailed a cab at the curb and said, "Take me to Jerusalem."

> When he arrived in Jerusalem, he said. "Take me to the jail that is holding the American prisoner." When Jackson got to the jail, he said, "Take me to the American prisoner." For some reason, they took him to the cell block. "Take me to the American's cell," he said. When he got to the cell door, he said to the guard, "Open the door."

The guard did so. Jackson walked into the cell and said to the American, "Come with me, we're going home." And the two of them walked out.

That kind of commitment in every moment—taking the next step in the right direction toward a compelling goal, for a compelling passion, for the public good—that energy is felt by others. And not always, but sometimes, it opens doors. And sometimes, although not always, it overcomes impossible odds.

It is that commitment to forward motion—also evidenced in the story of Ernest Shackleton getting his 27 men "all home alive" after their ship the *Endurance* was crushed in the ice-pack in Antarctica in 1915 – that so touches me. It is unstoppable energy.

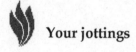 **Your jottings**

And while we may think of this alive energy as the energy of one remarkable person—Jesse Jackson or Ernest Shackleton.—it is also a collective energy, held in a group by the whole of the group. That sense prompted a poem "Only one" as I worked with a group of Texas executives:

The Art and Spirit of Leadership
judybrown@aol.com www.judysorumbrown.com

Only one

Only one
of twenty-six
was missing
when we gathered.
As a matter
of the math,
not so significant,
but somehow
we were whole again,
complete,
when he appeared.
The heart
has its own ways
of measuring.

Judy Brown, February 21, 2007

I have come to understand that leadership and life require knowing that there is a unique quality to each live encounter, a mystery, an unpredictability about what may lie around the next corner, when we choose to stay alive to the moment. And a messiness. To follow the alive moment, to hold onto the thread, requires that we know what is alive for us and that we also can see what is unique in the circumstance and the people around us.

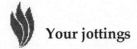 **Your jottings**

Never the same

Just now,
watching the fire burn
in this old fireplace
where I grew up,
I thought of logs
and people
and the things we build,
the work we do together.

That work, like building fires –
like this fire here and now –
lies in our sensing people
as we sense the logs:
How they'll fit into
this one fire,
the one right here,
right now;
feeling their weight,
their shape,
sensing how dry or green,
placing each one just so
and watching for a while
to see how that one works.

Does it catch easily
and there,
where I have put it?
Or does it need adjusting,
slightly?

Never the fire the same.
Never the logs.

Judy Brown, December 5, 2006

The Art and Spirit of Leadership
judybrown@aol.com www.judysorumbrown.com

As I look back over the threads of this set of musings, I am aware that if we are to follow the threads of aliveness, we must set aside our longing for neatness, certitude and predictability. The alive encounter, the threads of aliveness, the experiences of being human are of necessity mysterious and raggedy. I struggle with that awareness. The part of me that is the poet gets it. The rest of me isn't so sure.

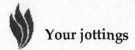 **Your jottings**

The Art and Spirit of Leadership
judybrown@aol.com   www.judysorumbrown.com

The poet spirit

The poet spirit's lost
in all the doings of the material world.
The ghost of poetry
glides silent
through the house,
among the lists
of things to do,
the neatly arranged rooms,
the shelves of books.
The poet spirit
looks for something
immaterial and messy
to snuggle up against,
to sniff,
to nuzzle,
to explore.

Judy Brown, January 20, 2003

The Art and Spirit of Leadership
judybrown@aol.com   www.judysorumbrown.com

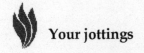 **Your jottings**

The Art and Spirit of Leadership
judybrown@aol.com   www.judysorumbrown.com

Chapter Eleven

Risk Speaking In Your Natural Voice

There is joy in the sound of human voices. The true tones. The variety of intonations. The natural rise and fall of sounds. One at a time. In twos. In hundreds.

Yet the natural sound is too rarely heard. Instead, we hear carefully controlled voices. Proper voices. Professional voices. People speaking in a syntax, a dialect, that is not their own, not their first language. Or we experience the heavy silence of those sorting out whether to speak at all.

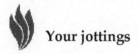 **Your jottings**

Voices

Voices,
like waves
on a beach,
the sounds
rising
and falling
across the room
of hundreds
of sojourners,
laughter
like sea froth,
tossed,
tossed,
and low voices
underneath
like thunder.

Judy Brown, June 24, 2008

It is a challenge, I think, to translate the corporate story, the story of the cause we serve, into our own language. To speak it with our authentic voice in a natural tone. To translate the purpose or the mission into the language of our heart, of our experience, of our calling. To give it human voice.

I find myself untouched by so many of today's policy arguments, stripped of the natural voice, even those policies I most strongly endorse. They are lifeless, tinny in tone. The example that comes most quickly to mind is in the environmental field, which repeatedly broadcasts anxious, angry and aggressive statements about the dire circumstances before us. No doubt all true. And continually reminding us of the importance of keeping land in its natural state. Without question, true. And yet, these calls for outrage and action fail. They fail to engage. They particularly fail to connect with those not already allied with their cause.

I think, in contrast, of Brian Price who founded and heads the land conservancy effort in the county where I grew up. I think of his ability to tell the natural, authentic human story of the tracts of land the Conservancy seeks to preserve. In doing so he carries forward the voices that have belonged to that land. One piece of land, Clay Cliffs, is the last stretch of open land reaching from the inland lake up across the hills to the Lake Michigan bluffs. Its original owner has died, and his family is working with the Conservancy to preserve the land.

Years ago, while sitting at a picnic table at a little park across the lake from Clay Cliffs, looking over at his property, the owner had remarked pensively to Brian, "Wouldn't it be wonderful if somehow it could all be preserved, so that like now, you could look across at it, at dusk, and not see a single light." Last week's newspaper from home carries the picture of that last stretch of open land. The headline, a single word marking a victory in land preservation: "Ours." All of ours.

The Art and Spirit of Leadership
judybrown@aol.com   www.judysorumbrown.com

It is these stories, these voices, that lend a sense of meaning and depth to environmental stewardship. Too often our work, our professions, and our roles leave us feeling as though we have been given a script stripped of our voice and personal inflection. We often use the term "professionalism" to describe that voice. It is our "professional" self. We've forgotten that the very word "professional" comes from the term "profess" that is, to give voice to what we believe deeply. Instead, we often find ourselves trapped in roles not unlike that of telemarketers who call us with a rote speech, mechanical and unstoppable.

Too often we fall into a pattern of speaking as if we were the disembodied voice of some entity that is not us. We speak dismissively of the corporate "line," about having to be politically correct. We complain about not being able to speak of what is really on our minds because of the risk to us. As one organization put it, because of the dangers of our words (or the judgment of others about our words) ending up in the "hall file."

In contrast, when we become passionate about a cause, our work, our calling, making the story our own, the voice our own true voice, we can speak from the heart about why the work matters to us.

It is the story spoken from the heart about purpose that is passed person to person and remembered. Such is the one about the janitor in the heart-transplant hospital in Texas who, when asked what he does there, says to a reporter that he and the famous doctor save lives. Or we tell the story of another janitor who, when asked what he did at Cape Canaveral, responds that he and NASA put astronauts into space.

These stories touch us because we recognize the truth in them, the wisdom of the person who can speak of the ways in which his work makes a profound difference in the world. Always in these stories there is feeling, emotion, caring and commitment. Our natural voice brings much more life and power to our work, to our organizations, to our communities.

If we can't find similar emotion within us, then we can't find our real voice. Voice is not about technique. Our real, natural voice has "timbre," life, emotion to it. It's why people turn their heads, and listen, when we speak.

I return to the wisdom and discipline of the woodcarver, who transforms the prince's command to create a bell stand into a work of art that shines with his own genius. It is a work of art that delights the prince and the assembled crowds alike. Then the woodcarver speaks directly and honestly to the gathered crowd, explaining how he has done the work that they attribute to the spirits. Explains it simply. Modestly. Precisely. In his own words. He explains how he has forgotten the command entirely, has forgotten the prince and his court, by freeing himself of anything that might distract him from the work that is his to do.

When Al Tervalon and I worked together in Ford's manufacturing plants, he, who eventually headed the quality control initiative, would talk with the people on the plant floor about the integrity of their product. Sometimes he got pretty emotional about the matter, too. He'd talk with tears in his eyes about why he cared so much about zero defects.

Certainly there was a corporate initiative to continually improve quality, and as certainly, those improvements drove plant profits, but that wasn't what was on his mind, nor in his words.

Al's heart-felt driven focus on quality came from a more direct and simple place, close to his heart. Perfect quality mattered because his mother and his wife both drove Ford products and their lives were in the hands of the guys on the plant floor. His emotions were real. And the guys knew it.

Al's directness, emotion and the realness of his voice transformed the quality issue from a corporate initiative to a close-to-the-bone issue for others as well—they too drove Ford products. Like Al, their families' safety relied on perfect quality.

When we speak directly from our own experience, from our heart, engaged in what matters most, others "hear" us, and they connect with what is real for us and what is real for them. They too begin to have the courage to speak in the same whole way.

Mary Oliver in her oft-quoted poem "The Journey" speaks of the power of recognizing our voice, the voice that keeps us, as she says, "company." Her words parallel those of Derek Walcott in his poem "Love after Love" when he talks of the one who "has loved you all your life." Both poets are pointing us towards the part of ourselves that is our essential, true self. That true self is always with us, although not always heard. The poets remind us of the power of hearing our natural, human voice, the one that feels like such a risk to "let speak."

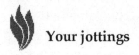 **Your jottings**

I recall moments in which my voice has spoken with such unexpected clarity, authority and power that I was tempted to look over my shoulder to ask, "Who said that?" The very first poem I wrote had that unexpected quality of voice. It startled me, scared me even:

Rebirth

And we will sell no more
of our eternity
in payment for dead dreams,
for denial of our losses,
but we will speak of loss
and of rebirth,
and we will treasure
gifts which are our own.

The time of this travail has passed,
and when another comes,
we will recall,
as if from ancient tribal story
that which we have come to know.

And when the cost of our belonging
is denial of an older truth,
when we're required
to set aside that which we've learned
through fire, to be true,
we will then recognize
this is no longer as we hoped,
the circle of our spirit,
and with deep sadness and necessity

The Art and Spirit of Leadership
judybrown@aol.com   www.judysorumbrown.com

we will then turn our face
once more toward the path
and journey on until we come
to that new place
where our true story
can be spoken
around yet another tribal fire.

This know we
now and always.
Let the earth
remind us
when the storms
around us
overwhelm
the tiny, still
voice of truth within.

Judy Brown, Summer 1993, Maine.

The Art and Spirit of Leadership
judybrown@aol.com   www.judysorumbrown.com

The experience of this first poem, showing up in my journal years ago, shook me. It was like a huge thunderclap right over my head. Yet it took me years to recognize the voice as my own, and it has kept me company throughout all the times since. Times of many changes, transitions, ups and downs.

As I write this, I am struck by the unerring guidance that our natural, authentic voice can provide. Terrifying and unsettling perhaps, but unerring. That first poem was written in my journal as I sat before a huge stone fireplace in a beautiful post and beam three-story home my then husband and I had designed and had had built by local crafts people in Maine. He still owns it, and the children, adults now, gather there each August.

Here, today, I write before a similarly beautiful fieldstone fireplace, this one in my childhood home in Michigan, built by a gifted Michigan stone-mason. He had done the work on it after we left last year, so we saw it for the first time when we arrived recently for our annual visit. In a way, this is the fireplace this old lake cottage should have always had. I'm stunned by its beauty—the varying colors, shapes, textures and sizes of the Michigan field stone. Some of the stones were picked from the rock pile out behind the garage, left there when Dad dug the basement underneath the old cottage, by hand back in the 40's. Real.

Last night my husband and I sat for a long time, studying the fireplace. Noticing the range of colors and shapes: blues, pinks, grays, huge rocks a foot across, smaller ones, one shaped like a loaf of homemade peasant bread, two or three with streaks through them of a different hue. If you run your hand over the stones, some are surprisingly soft, smooth, others grainy, rough. Voices are like that. Individual. Each different. Beautiful together, yet still individual, when drawn into a single work of art—as are these stones in this fireplace.

The Art and Spirit of Leadership
judybrown@aol.com www.judysorumbrown.com

I begin to see that the fireplace is made up of circles of stones, a center stone ringed by 6 or 7 others. And then, after sitting for a long time studying the fireplace, I realize that often one of the "ring" stones is the center stone in another circle. So with leadership—sometimes we are the center voice, the convening voice, the framing voice. Sometimes we say something, either by role or wisdom, that gives new shape to the effort. And sometimes we are just one in the circle, part of the dialogue, yet no less important for being one of many.

The practice of speaking from our natural voice requires knowing that voice, recognizing it, treasuring it. We must practice with it, as with any instrument, so we have the courage to be present publicly with that very real, authentic voice. I am reminded of the message I take from the work of Pamela Siegel, who is studying voice seriously, practicing and singing publicly. Now sufficiently comfortable with her practice, she is able to lead others in "rounds" where they hear themselves and can hear others.

And I think of my colleague and voice coach Claude Stein leading groups of executives through an exercise in which they sing a song about a place that means a great deal to them. Small groups of four executives, sitting knee to knee in a room, each one creating a song about a place, and singing it, haltingly, sometimes "Johnny one-note style" but nonetheless singing it to three colleagues. It is an exercise in risk taking, willing to be in our own authentic voice about something that really matters to us. Having the courage to sing in public.

"Lift every voice and sing," the anthem of the civil rights movement, comes to mind. What does it mean to "lift every voice?" How do we create conditions where we encourage others to join in, to "lift" every voice?

Over the years, one of the most powerful examples of voice and courage, for me, remains Martin Luther King's letter written in

The Art and Spirit of Leadership
judybrown@aol.com   www.judysorumbrown.com

1963 from a Birmingham city jail cell. Whenever I am feeling constrained, helpless or scared, and therefore afraid to speak out, I take a lesson from King. First, I ask myself whether I have practiced the capacity to think clearly enough to know what is on my mind. Then, I ask if I have the courage and discipline to actually "write the letter," to put pen to paper, fingers to keyboard, or to speak my piece. And finally, am I willing to send the letter? The letter is my perspective, my truth—not with a capital "T" but with a small "t"—my contribution to our collective understanding, my piece of the puzzle.

I remind myself of what King faced: writing from a jail cell no bigger than a couple of conference tables, facing uncertainty along with the violence and hatred of his jailers, without a single book for reference or comfort, and only the margins of *The New York Times* and toilet-paper on which to write. Yet King is in full voice as he lays out a stunningly powerful case for his commitment to non-violent action in the cause of universal civil rights. Although many of us are familiar with his ringing voice in the now-famous "I Have a Dream" speech delivered in Washington DC, I think it is this letter written from a Birmingham, Alabama jail cell, which is an even more powerful representation of his voice.

Perhaps it is the range of King's voice in his letter to the clergymen who are urging him to "chill"—a voice range that includes emotion, stories, Biblical citations, genius-level reframing ("Was not Jesus an extremist for love?"), analogies, philosophy, reason, humor—it is all there. A *tour de force*. Voice in full range. All the octaves. Personal and timeless.

But you and I are mere mortals, and I suppose it's natural to hide behind the notion that "I am not Martin Luther King nor am I Gandhi"—when we are feeling scared, small, uncertain and insignificant. Yet no matter who we are or where we are or how we are feeling, we can always hold to the practice of speaking our authentic truth as clearly as we know how. And we can

The Art and Spirit of Leadership
judybrown@aol.com   www.judysorumbrown.com

remember that doing so may influence others, educate others, in ways we can never know. The impact of our authentic voice is unpredictable.

We can't know what reactions or judgments or possibilities might unfold from speaking our truth. Nor when. But that is not our business. As Martha Graham would remind us, it is our business only to keep the channel clear. The channel is our voice.

When what we say comes from a place of depth, of commitment, of experience, of a hard-won personal truth, our voice carries like the last note of a great symphony hanging in the air. It has resonance, a memorable and lasting power.

I remember one such conversation that helped me make a necessary change in my life. The words were so clear, so powerful that they seem to reverberate across time and space, affecting not only my life but the lives of others with whom I have shared the story. The speaker: my mentor John Gardner.

I had been talking with Gardner, complaining gracelessly actually, about my job with an organization that should have been a perfect fit for me, and wasn't. I was increasingly miserable at work, but I prided myself on not giving up. On being able to handle anything. Quite a silly idea, on reflection. After listening quietly to my litany of woes, John was silent for a while and then he said, simply, "It's important to know when to leave."

Those simple words: "It's important to know when to leave," were not what I expected. Nor were they quite what I wanted to hear. But I could sense the profound truth in them. The quiet and real emotion.

There was something about the simplicity of his words, the silence from which he spoke, and the tone, that went straight to my heart. It took me 18 months to move into action and leave the organization. But the path was revealed in the moment of the quiet ringing tone of his words.

I wrote of that conversation in an earlier book of reflections on my father's life. Quoted Gardner exactly. One day a colleague called me to say that he was leaving an organization where he had worked for decades. He wanted me to know how he had arrived at his decision. "I was reading your book," he said, "the part where John Gardner says to you 'It's important to know when to leave.' And in that moment I knew it was time to go. I think my family thought I was making an unnecessary change, but I knew. I had to leave." Twice he called me to reiterate that experience with Gardner's words. So the next time I saw John, I told him of the power of those words. He took in what I said, but said nothing in reply.

Only many years later did I learn of the life experience that lay behind Gardner's words to me that day. Gardner himself had once made a very difficult decision to leave. Serving as the only Republican in Lyndon Johnson's cabinet (as Secretary of Health Education and Welfare), he was in the midst of exhilarating work at a national level on issues that mattered greatly to him. He was presiding over monumental changes in the health care system and helping shape the civil rights legislation that opened educational opportunities for minority students. The job of a lifetime.

But as the season neared for LBJ to launch his re-election campaign, Gardner found himself increasingly troubled by the President's policies in Vietnam. He asked to meet with LBJ at his Texas ranch and in a quiet conversation explained that he had grave reservations about Vietnam. He believed that a president who was seeking re-election deserved the wholehearted support of everyone on his cabinet. Gardner, himself a Marine, who revered LBJ's domestic accomplishments, could not support his Vietnam policy. So he told the President that he would resign on Monday, giving as his reason that he wished to move on to other opportunities. That Monday, Gardner resigned from his dream position. Three weeks later, President Johnson announced that he would not seek re-election.

I realize now, as I could not have then, that when John said, "It's important to know when to leave," he was speaking from deep and painful experience and from the depths of the dilemma that he had felt as he walked away from his cabinet position.

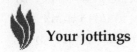 **Your jottings**

The Art and Spirit of Leadership
judybrown@aol.com   www.judysorumbrown.com

Truth

Speaking
truth to power,
love to friendship,
pain to those whose
words and acts have prompted it,
bears no relationship
to how the world responds.

It is the gold
of our own truth
we offer freely,
as if a gift,
with no consideration,
no expectation,
of return.

Judy Brown, March 16, 2004

Another reminder of the power and importance of authentic voice, of equal impact but in a quite different way, has been, for me, the simple visual of the *Cone in the Box* that my colleague Bob Ginnett sketched on a blackboard in Colorado, years ago.

In the years since, I have shared Bob's simple sketch of the cone in the box with dozens of groups. In retreats. In keynotes. In leadership classes. In workshops on dialogue. The lesson for me, is that what we see is essential, and it is essential that we speak of it. And also that 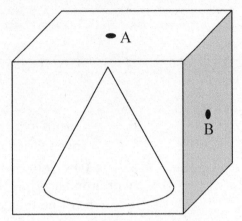 what we see is not the whole picture. It is both accurate and partial. Speaking out about what we see from our vantage point is essential to the stewardship of what we most care about. But, equally important is drawing out the perspectives of others who do not sit where we sit, and who see something different.

When someone talks over another, debates the other into silence or uses power to silence another point of view, they put our lives at risk. But even more powerful for me has been the notion that when I refuse to say what I see, because I am shy, uncertain, don't want to cause trouble or ruffle feathers, I also put our lives at risk. *Cone in the Box* instills an ethic of authentic voice and a deep and abiding curiosity about the perspective of others who see things differently. It is an ethic of inviting in each person's authentic voice.

I think, too, that it may be hard for us to recognize our own authentic voice. Sometimes others hear it with greater fidelity. And call it out. Increasingly for me, the voice is in my poetry.

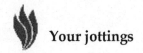 **Your jottings**

But it has not always been so. Years back, when I was writing a book on reflective leadership practice, a colleague from one of the manufacturing plants called me. He went by his last name only: Berdish. He called because he'd heard that I was writing a leadership book and he wanted to make sure the book included a poem I'd written for the guys in the plant: "Trust equals speed."

"Berdish," I said, exasperated. "This is a serious leadership book, not a poetry book. Prose not poetry. No poetry."

"Look," he said, "You did a lot of good stuff for us in the plants, but the most important thing you ever did was to write us that poem about trust equals speed. PUT IT IN THE BOOK." And Berdish hung up.

I put it in the book.

The Art and Spirit of Leadership
judybrown@aol.com   www.judysorumbrown.com

Trust equals speed

"Trust equals speed," he said
explaining why we need
to trust at work. Trust
lets us move ahead
with lightening speed.
I think he's right.

Yet trust takes time.
It's silent, too,
and meditative in its
steps. It moves at
paces that seem slow
and hesitating,
first one foot,
then the next.

Trust is a dance
developed over time,
a set of natural steps
emerging from a bond
forged from the passion
that we feel for dreams
we hold in common,
and respect
for all the ways we're not alike,
both held, the dreams and difference,
unflinching and aware,
day after day,
as we work
side by side.

The Art and Spirit of Leadership
judybrown@aol.com www.judysorumbrown.com

Trust equals speed.
Yet it is utterly,
completely still.
Trust is unmoving
and it is the speed
of light.

Judy Brown, September 12, 1997

The Art and Spirit of Leadership
judybrown@aol.com www.judysorumbrown.com

It was Berdish's insistence that the poem go into the leadership book that started me along the path of poetry, prose, principles and practices all woven together. I was forced into it, because someone else could hear my true voice in a way I could not.

The Universe keeps sending me reminders about poetry and voice. Over dinner recently, a colleague who works with people living with AIDS, told me of a women's group that gathers regularly with whom she had shared my poetry. They found it helpful. That delighted me. But even more surprising to me was when she forgot my poetry book at one gathering and turned instead to another poet, the women's reaction was immediate: "That's not the poetry you usually bring us. We want the poetry by that other woman." Even strangers in Florida can hear when it is really my voice. The words carry across space and over time.

Sometimes our authentic voice speaks in an unemotional way, simply reporting on what we have seen. In doing so, it drops a pebble in a large pond, and the ripples carry it far and wide. I learned this in a surprising way from a simple administrative action I took years back.

> The first day I ever went house-shopping, was in Lansing, Michigan in the late 60's. The realtor, eager for a sale was quite friendly and said "This is a wonderful neighborhood, very stable."
>
> "What do you mean," I asked, honestly innocent.
>
> "It's all White," he said, "and it will stay that way."
>
> "How do you know that?" I asked, much less innocently.
>
> "Well," he continued in his naturally friendly manner, "if a Black family were interested in this house, the price would be much higher, and it would have to be all cash."

As he chattered on, I asked him for his card. I walked out of the house and calmly proceeded to the housing authority and filed a report of housing discrimination, figuring they probably got reports like this all the time, and my report would not have much impact. But I figured that as a citizen, I should report what I had seen. It was a simple thing to do. A straight-forward administrative act. And it took no particular courage. Just time and attention.

As it turns out, they didn't get such reports all the time. In fact, this was the first time a white-skinned person had filed a charge of discrimination "on behalf" of a dark-skinned person. Suddenly the realtors could no longer assume they could judge their "pitch" on the color of someone's skin. It changed everything. And it was a very simple thing to do.

We need to remember that sometimes the simple act of reporting what we see, an act taken because the inner voice says, "It's the right thing to do," can move mountains, at least small ones.

The poet Nikki Giovanni tells the story of visiting with her elder, the civil rights leader Rosa Parks. Rosa was the person of color who refused to move to the back of the bus when ordered to do so, consequently sparking a famous incident that accelerated the pace of civil rights changes in the south.

"Rosa," Giovanni asked one day, "the day you refused to move, there must have been other people on that bus who did move to the back of the bus."

"Oh yes," said Rosa, "there were."

"Well, how did you feel about that, about your sitting and taking the risk, and them moving to the back of the bus?"

 The Art and Spirit of Leadership
judybrown@aol.com   www.judysorumbrown.com

Rosa's response has stayed with me, indelibly: "Well, there were people on that bus who had responsibilities that made them feel it was impossible to chance losing a day's pay, or ending up in jail. I knew that. But I knew that this was the day I could take a stand. So I did."

This is always the leadership question for me: "Is this the day I can take a stand? Speak truth to power? Am I the one whose turn it is? Will I recognize my own authentic voice, and will it ring true for others?"

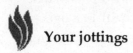 **Your jottings**

Chapter 12

Take Care Of Yourself; You Are A Treasure

As each of us gains more clarity about what makes our heart sing and the world we hope to nurture into being, we face the challenge of caring for ourselves with the same intention and sense of commitment that we show towards the other causes and commitments in our lives.

It is easy to fall into habits of pushing ourselves far beyond the healthy limits of our mental, spiritual and physical energy. It is easy to forget that rest is restorative. That spirit needs space to renew itself. That the mind needs time to meander, to wander, to wonder. That our health is a resource not just to us but to the causes and people we care about.

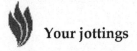 **Your jottings**

Maintaining perspective about these dimensions of our lives is a life-long assignment in being self-aware. The world challenges us continuously, tempts us to overwork, to ignore the limits inherent in the human system. Tempts us to disconnect from life's joys and the nourishment and restorative powers they offer. Whatever path allows us to remember that we are a treasure for which we serve as steward, that path calls to us:

judybrown@aol.com   www.judysorumbrown.com

Poet space

These are the days
of poet space—
no plans,
no pressure,
no anxieties,
only bare awareness,
letting the spirit
roam unleashed,
unfettered,
free, curious, alive,
sniffing the air
for life,
nostrils flared,
still and aware.

Judy Brown, September 5, 2010

The Art and Spirit of Leadership
judybrown@aol.com www.judysorumbrown.com

The world gives us cues and clues all the time about the importance of balance and self-care, if we take the time to notice those cues and clues.

Last spring, over the course of dashing about in a rambling hotel where a several-day meeting was taking place, I took a "short-cut" out the front door and around through the tulip garden, then back in a side door. My short-cut gave me a soul-renewing burst of fresh April air, sunlight and glorious spring flowers. I felt as though I'd been inside for days. I was in the process of congratulating myself on this small victory of self-care, when I spotted something that stopped me in my tracks.

There, in the middle of the large, flat, bricked entryway, the area where taxis disgorge passengers, where people arrive dragging their baggage, where the bell-men congregate to welcome guests, there, at my feet lay a large squirrel, perhaps 18 inches long from the tip of its pink nose to the very end of its tail, stretched out fully, face down, on the bricks, front legs splayed out ahead, back legs stretched out behind, flat on its stomach, tail straight out behind.

At first glance, I thought the squirrel was dead. Yuck! But as I stood still and watched, I could see the animal was breathing. And there was no sign of injury.

I thought "Maybe the squirrel is sick, or even worse, rabid." But there was no frothing at the mouth, and no sign of sickness. Just the squirrel stretched out on the red brick, breathing. And not moving. I stood and watched. Nothing happened. No movement. The squirrel didn't move. I didn't move.

I waved the head bell-man over and pointed at the squirrel at my feet. "Look," I said. "Oh, don't worry," replied the bellman seemingly unsurprised by what I'd pointed out. "She won't hurt you."

The Art and Spirit of Leadership
judybrown@aol.com   www.judysorumbrown.com

I explained I wasn't worried for me, I was worried for the squirrel. Somebody might step on her or run over her. "Oh," he said, "it's not a problem." "She does this all the time. She comes here to rest. We think she's pregnant. See, she's pretty fat. So she rests here. It's not a problem."

The bellman walked away, as if this were absolutely a sensible arrangement — the one between him and the squirrel.

My mind returns to that scene again and again. The squirrel resting on the brick entryway and the bellman not at all troubled that, in his work space, a living critter was taking care of herself.

I think how seldom we are as wise as the squirrel. And how even less often we are as wise as the bellman. To consider that this squirrel-nap was "no problem" and to arrange work around her.

This scene is so unlike the gerbil wheels that we get ourselves trapped on and create for others. Ignoring the need for the human spirit to rest. The need for time out.

A colleague spoke to me of the sabbatical she took about a decade ago — a sabbatical in a profession where such an arrangement is rare, almost unheard of. Practically as unusual as a squirrel napping in a hotel entryway. "When I came back from the sabbatical, I never again got back into that frantic pace that had once seemed so natural and so required," she said.

So a sabbatical, a Sabbath, a time out, can do more than just restore our energies. It can reshape entirely what we see as necessary, as required, in the way we expend our energy.

It changes how we define our worth in the world. At some level, it can help us begin to believe that we ourselves are worthy of the same quality of attention that we give to others.

The Art and Spirit of Leadership
judybrown@aol.com   www.judysorumbrown.com

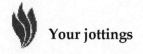 **Your jottings**

The Art and Spirit of Leadership
judybrown@aol.com   www.judysorumbrown.com

Retreat

Each of us
holds a thread
of some vast tapestry
that we can't
know alone.
It is in that awareness
that we gather
here together,
laying down
our burdens,
lifting up
the threads.

Judy Brown, March 21, 2008

How can we remain centered and in a space of sabbatical, of retreat, of relative equanimity in the face of all that the world tosses at us? How do we avoid the energy drain created by our own reactivity to everything that comes our way? It is so easy, particularly when we are exhausted, to get ginned up, as I often say, to get ourselves "wrapped around the axle" about what we see going on.

My friend Gary Glenna, CEO of a Minneapolis firm and a long-time pilot, called me one day out of the blue to tell me a story about flying and how we unknowingly create our own turbulence, our own rough weather. How we participate actively and heavily in our own exhaustion.

> Gary, who pilots his own twin-engine plane, learned when he was a novice pilot, that turbulence often comes from our way of reacting to the world around us. He would go out to log some flying time on a day of beautiful, calm weather. After he'd been flying for 15 minutes or so, he would notice it was getting a bit bumpy. Before too long, it was quite turbulent. So, he'd come down and land, and pick up a conversation with one of the much more experienced pilots.
>
> "Bumpy up there," Gary would say.
>
> "No," the other would say. "Perfectly calm."
>
> Puzzled, Gary began to learn from the more experienced pilots that if you respond to every move the airplane makes, each of your moves creates another move on the part of the plane to which you then react by making another move. Before you know it, you are flying in turbulence entirely of your own making.

I remember days like that in my own life.

The Art and Spirit of Leadership
judybrown@aol.com   www.judysorumbrown.com

Gary's piloting advice has stayed with me—front and center in my mind, and heart. By being always on the ready, always reacting, I create a world which demands increasing amounts of my constant attention. I find myself in a weather system of my own making.

So now I ask myself, "How is it that by reacting, by caring, by helping, by stepping in, by taking action—all good things in themselves—I am generating the turbulence? How much of what I experience as the unexpected "weather" of my life is simply a matter of trying to over-control, and over-direct the light airplane that is my life?"

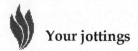 **Your jottings**

Hummingbirds asleep

When do the humming birds
get naps? When do they sleep?
The tiny helicopter-birds,
buzzing about their busy business
all day long are nowhere to be found
at four fifteen
with dawn an hour away.

When they're at rest, they're gone.
Evaporated. They don't exist.
It's only busyness, activity
gives them their visibility,
their realness in our eyes.

Maybe we think the same of us.
Without our work,
activity,
we disappear.
Or so we fear.

Judy Brown Aug 22, 2000
Aspen, Colorado

The Art and Spirit of Leadership
judybrown@aol.com www.judysorumbrown.com

Time to Reflect

The joys of the life I lead now — and the relative equanimity I am able to more frequently muster — lead to a more expansive and less reactive approach to challenges. This was, in part, a result of the wisdom handed me by a CEO I met nearly a decade ago. Her name is Jennie Chin Hansen, and she was part of a group of leaders in the field of services to the elderly who gathered annually to reflect, renew and learn together. They had, over the years, been determined to keep this time of retreat, despite heavy leadership responsibilities and multiple demands on their time.

These leaders invited me to spend a day with them exploring the principles and practices of transformational leadership. A day about leaders who change things for the better, leaders who innovate in ways that transform their field. It was one of those invitations that made my heart sing. And it was in Florida during the winter. An easy yes.

Over the course of our day together, we found our way into a conversation about burn-out and how easy, even likely, it becomes in a field that focuses on caring for others. How can leaders avoid the long hours that lead to burn-out?

Jennie said that the only way she knew to stay healthy and renewed was to always know where her next vacation would be. That idea took me by surprise. I was a single mom at that point, with a daughter just heading off to college, and I never even thought about vacations. I carried responsibilities solo, and I worked. And I mothered. Sometimes we visited family in one place or another or planned something special for Meg and her friends. But a vacation for me? Planned? Unheard of. Something about what Jennie said and the clarity and simplicity of it, got under my skin, and into my head. And wouldn't go away.

The Art and Spirit of Leadership
judybrown@aol.com   www.judysorumbrown.com

I flew home from that retreat, recalling that Roger, a good friend from my days in the auto industry in Detroit, had offered me a chance to use his condo in Turks and Caicos for a vacation. Free. My reaction at the time, months back, had been to politely thank him, but to make a mental note that my life had no place for vacations, and besides I didn't even know where Turks and Caicos was. I was a hard-working mom, not an island girl.

But Jennie's comment rattled around in my head, louder and louder. So I took a deep breath and e-mailed Roger:

> "Roger, remember your offer of your place in Turks and Caicos?"

> "Judy. I remember. The offer stands."

> "Roger, is it available….." and I filled in the dates of Meg's spring break when she would be going off on a trip with her girlfriends.

> "Judy, yes it is."

> "Roger, I'll take it."

Long pause between e-mails, and then reality kicked in.

> "Roger, does it have internet; and fax; and will my cell phone come in? And does it have a coffee maker? And how far is it from the beach?"

> "Judy, my friend David, who is resident manager there, will answer all your questions and he will meet your plane. I've copied him on this email. David meet Judy. Judy meet David."

Roger disappeared from the exchange, and I was e-mailing a stranger named David in a place called Turks and Caicos which was Heaven only knew where.

So I, a practical northerner, flew to a Caribbean island destination with my suitcase and a wadded up e-mail with the phone number of Roger's friend David.

David who had moved to a warm island after 34 years in England and 24 years in Canada, swearing he would never again shovel snow or cut grass, is now a permanent resident of the US (my fourth country, he calls it). Later, he and I would accuse Roger of match-making, and Roger would deny having any role in our romance, engagement, marriage.

Should you think this a fairy-tale romance and story, we wish to add a few details about the ups and downs of a commuting relationship, including my worries when Hurricane Frances struck the Turks and Caicos, and only David and Roger remained to madly remove porch screens so that the winds wouldn't tear the porches off the condos. By some miracle the phones worked throughout the entire ordeal, although everything else was out, and the airport was closed. I had a play-by-play of the excitement—and began to wonder about the wisdom of island living.

And then there were the border problems that stemmed from David entering the US to marry me without having a special visa to marry a US citizen. (We had no idea there was such a thing!) We found out about it when David was stopped at the Canadian border, and Homeland Security closed the border to him until he had one. "How long does it take to get one?" he asked innocently enough. "Six months," was the answer. And the officer ran both David's passports through the system and did indeed close the border to him. He had crossed the border alone, while I was at work in northern Michigan. We thought he'd be gone a couple of

The Art and Spirit of Leadership
judybrown@aol.com   www.judysorumbrown.com

hours. It was May 15th. It would be the first of October before the "fiancée visa" would be approved, and he could cross back into the US. In the meantime, he lived in Ontario with his daughter Lucinda and her partner Tony (an extreme case of guess who is coming to dinner and staying for an indeterminate time).

The June 25th wedding was postponed. And when David reentered the US, he did so with a visa that said he was coming into the country to marry Judith Ann Brown (not just anyone) and that if we didn't get married within 90 days, they would throw him out again. So we organized a joyous wedding within six weeks of his arrival back in the States.

Since all this happened after the events of September 11, 2001 had produced stricter security rules, we had border crossing problems for years thereafter. One of the standard border crossing questions is, "Have you ever been denied entrance to the US" and if your answer is "yes," it's good for about a two hour delay. But finally, David's "green card" was issued. ("The green card isn't green, but then red tape isn't red," said a friend.) After we'd been married for two years and had provided documents and letters from friends saying that our marriage was not a sham to get him into the US, the border crossings became quite easy.

But we still approach the border between the US and Canada with some sense of trepidation. A few days ago, at the border crossing at Sarnia, Ontario, on our way from Lucinda and Tony's to the family cottage in Michigan, we sailed through with pleasure, patting ourselves on the back about how all was well and the border troubles were in the past. David was driving the red Mustang, and I shuffled the passports to make sure the agent had put David's green card back in his passport. IT WAS MISSING! We now well knew that the green card is an absolute requirement to leave the US and to enter it.

The Art and Spirit of Leadership
judybrown@aol.com   www.judysorumbrown.com

My mind flashed ahead to our plans--to drive through Canada on the way home from Michigan, David's plan to take his daughter to England for their family reunion. All required a green card. My panicked mind was already on plan B—how to get a replacement green card fast from a cottage in northern Michigan without having to do a day's drive to Detroit or Chicago.

David put the car in reverse and backed it toward the American side of the border against oncoming traffic, (which looked very suspicious, of course) and into a parking spot next to a police officer at the border.

"You can't park there," the policeman said sternly, "What's the problem?" We explained.

"Go inside," he said sternly. We went inside, meekly. Soon he returned, "The agent says she gave the card back to you."

"We don't have it," I squawked. The police officer now had the passports, and it was clear the card was missing.

"I'll have an officer check your car," he said, and took the keys from David.

Now we had no passports, no green card, and no car keys. Not a good situation for people with our history.

After about 10 minutes, the police officer returned.

"Our officer found the card," he said pointing to a younger junior officer. "It had fallen between the passenger seat and the console."

The lanky young officer explained that it often happens—and that he'd had to move the passenger seat forward and back and look under the seat from every direction to find the card. Why he had been willing to take the extra time and effort to dig around for it was beyond me. He could so easily have said, "Sorry, it's not there."

We thanked him and went on our way. But the surprise of that experience stays with me. A federal police officer went out of his way to find something that would make such a difference to us, two strangers.

This experience, and others, remind me that part of caring for ourselves is to practice optimism, to realize that while the world is often a difficult place, there are islands of kindness, times that things do go well. There are oases of people working extra hard to make our lives easier, better. This can so easily be overlooked.

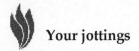 **Your jottings**

The story that we tell

The story that we tell
about how life must be—
can harden us to life's surprises,
to her gleeful serendipity.

The story that we tell
about what we must do
or be, or say,
deafens us to music
that is ours alone to play.

The story that we tell
about how life unfolds—
(the life that's ours, that is—)
puts us to sleep,
and so we miss the dawning
of our better world,
as we snooze on.

The Art and Spirit of Leadership
judybrown@aol.com   www.judysorumbrown.com

The story that we tell
about the balance we were meant to strike
among achievement
and the matters of the heart,
the causes that we care about,
the ones we're meant to love—
that balance isn't what we thought at all—
and we can't see that til we're thrown
into a hopeless
dizzied state of lost confusion.

The story that is ours
to live completely
is a mystery to us—
because we're busy telling ourselves stories
that no longer fit—
until we wake one day
and see life with our newly opened eyes,
full of surprise.

Judy Brown, May 29, 2001

The Art and Spirit of Leadership
judybrown@aol.com   www.judysorumbrown.com

Self-care is not necessarily a solitary endeavor. Although it generally requires some solitude, we can often find or create a community to support us in our renewal. With the same intention we create exercise groups, garden groups, or book clubs, we can gather together a group of friends who share our need for and discipline of renewal and self care. They can operate, much as my friend Paula Underwood described the role of Spider Woman in Native American lore: Spider Woman, she explained, stays up all night mending and repairing the damage that the world has done, during the day, to the web of connections.

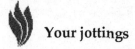 **Your jottings**

Paths

We are
each others
paths not taken.
We are
the stewards
of each others gifts.
Able to see
gems otherwise
unseen
in daytime's
harsher light,
we are
the harvest moon
for one another,
glowing in a sky
that turns toward
wintertime.

Judy Brown, May 4, 2008

The Art and Spirit of Leadership
judybrown@aol.com   www.judysorumbrown.com

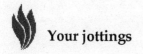 **Your jottings**

The Art and Spirit of Leadership
judybrown@aol.com   www.judysorumbrown.com

The Gift Of This Time

One of my favorite journal practices, one that I often build into dialogue work with groups, is to suggest we all take a quiet moment with the journal to complete this sentence stem: "This is a time in my life when...." In a way, I realize now, that writing this book, these chapters, has been a form of completing that sentence for myself. I invite you to do so as well.

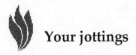 **Your jottings**

As I think of this time in my life, I realize how much it is about transformation—not just transformational leadership, which is a topic woven throughout these pages—but about life itself, the subtle transformations that often occur outside our awareness.

Transformed

We fall asleep
in the light of a full moon
through the trees.
While we sleep
nature changes her mind—
moonlight disappears,
rain, thunder, lightning
sweep through.
We know nothing
of the gradualness
of the transformation.
We sleep through
all the subtle signs.
Only the thunder
wakes us.
Suddenly
the world outside—
transformed—
takes us by surprise.

How many days?
How many nights
are just like that?
How often do we sleep
through subtleties
of transformation,
to then awake
surprised?

Judy Brown, April 4, 2007

I've been thinking back to the rental agent, Brian, who said of Meg's NYU Law School offer, "It's her dream. We couldn't think of standing in the way of her dream." He isn't just running a business, he is creating a world by the very spirit with which he approaches everything he does. And in doing so, he invites us to similarly help shape that world—a generous world—a connected world. A "Pass It Forward" world. To strangers, friends and family alike.

As we stand in line waiting to get into Meg's law school graduation, I slip a homeless man some money. I know everybody says not to do that. But it seems to be the right thing to do. Generosity from strangers. Generosity to strangers. And generosity to each other.

Despite all the advice to "Cut your kids off as soon as they are in their twenties so they can learn to sink or swim," I want to support Meg. Her dream is to provide legal aid to farmers who want to stay in sustainable farming in New York State. I want to support her dream to live in the city and serve farmers. Yes, it's unusual, but so was my idea, (dare I say "dream"?) to spend my summers flying between New York City and Europe.

Her dream is to increase the links between local food products, grown with sustainable practices, the people who can grow them, and the people who want to purchase them. To create links between the farmlands and the cities. Her idea, by an old logic, might seem impossible. But, by the logic of the world we are creating, a connected world, a world that values "local" and unique contributions, her dream can help create the world we want.

Legal aid for farmers. Not a massive farm bill in Congress but rather support for estate planning, dialogues about dreams, information on food regulations, and assistance creating sensible land lease arrangements. From the moment that Meg hatched the idea of a non-profit that would somehow make it possible for farmers, particularly young farmers, to stay on the land and farm in environmentally and economically sustainably ways, I've been thinking about how much my father, her grandfather, would be delighted at her idea.

Born into a Michigan farm family, my father was the County Agricultural Agent in Leelanau County, Michigan, a farming and fishing area along the northwestern shore of Lake Michigan. In his own way, in his own time, he worked to keep farmers farming. During the Depression, he had been a specialist for the Farm Security Administration, helping impoverished farmers keep their land during those very rough years. Then he shifted to the Agricultural Extension Service where, as an agronomist and small fruit specialist, he spent twenty-some years helping farmers develop more successful farms. He was constantly experimenting with new crops, new approaches, and new methods.

Meg's passion for the farm sustainability work comes not only from her grandfather and her DNA, but has also been spurred by the "foodie" culture of New York City and her fascination with the older rural processes: canning, the CSA movement—"But what can I do with all that chard?" she wails—and her realization that good legal advice could make a world of difference for young farmers and those worn out by farming who want to figure a way to turn the reins over to the next generation.

I watch this growing intent within her and realize that I am witness to the changing of leadership, the handing over of reins to a new generation of young leaders. Like my great mentor John Gardner, I feel myself settling into the role of being not so much a "do-er" with a "to-do" list, but increasingly an encourager, someone who watches for others' dreams and supports them in every way I can.

311

My husband says I am the poet of nature, that when I am in natural settings the poetry flows. True. True of our home along the Chesapeake's muddy tributaries. True of this old cottage where I grew up, along the brilliantly sparkling Lake Leelanau in northwest Michigan. I am a child of nature.

Once, years ago, in conversation with my therapist about the heavy responsibilities and pressures and demands I was experiencing, the stress that seemed to weigh me down from all directions, she tasked,

"And when did it start?"

My immediate answer: "When I was six."

Her question: "What happened then?"

My answer, "I went to school."

And what did you do before that, she asked, and I answered without missing a beat:

"I played in the woods."

My native habitat is the woods and all it represents—the beauty, the constant change and variability, the growth and the rot, the light raining down through the leaves.

My friend Roger, introducing me as a speaker at a conference on sustainability, said, "This is my friend Judy. She is a quirky poet." I was startled at the time, and also delighted.

Poets get to be quirky. They get to be whoever they are. And, it's been a long road getting there.

Quirky poets

Quirky poets
are ageless,
it dawns on me.
That's what
he called me,
"My friend,
a quirky poet."
Educators may
live past their prime.
Consultants tire.
Robert Frost was
a bad apple farmer
at the end.
But words he'd written—
they were ageless.

Judy Brown, April 1, 2007

The Art and Spirit of Leadership
judybrown@aol.com www.judysorumbrown.com

In that awareness, I realize that in an odd kind of way, I have written this book for myself. I have written it to listen to myself and to more clearly discern what makes my heart sing.

Meg just left to go back to NYC to study for the bar exam. Before she left, she discovered we had a woods full of leeks (called "ramps" in the NYC foodie culture), lush clumps of ramps growing in the eight acres of woodland behind this old cottage.

After a dinner of ramps and pasta (go figure, it was wonderful!), delighted with the results of her experiment, she and I and my husband found ourselves digging leeks in the increasing darkness, so she could pickle them before she left. We listened out of the corner of our consciousness to an oncoming thunderstorm. When the first crack of lightening struck about a mile away, we ran for the house, and dashed in laughing just before the downpour.

All this richness and discovery in the woods where I grew up, that I know like my own hand.

My land.

> Rumi says it best:
>
> Today, like every other day, we wake up empty
> and frightened. Don't open the door to the study
> and begin reading. Take down a musical instrument.
>
> Let the beauty we love be what we do.
> There are hundreds of ways to kneel and kiss the ground.

And I suppose if I were to think about the way to "kneel and kiss the ground" here and now, it would be reflected thus:

The Art and Spirit of Leadership
judybrown@aol.com www.judysorumbrown.com

Serving

I give to those
who wear themselves out
striving for
the general good,
tending the cause,
caring in loss,
determined,
driven, worn.

I give them space
in which to
rediscover hope.
I give them words
which turn them
to their need
to tend themselves.
I help them find
their gifts again.

I offer them
the simplest things:
Calm,
Presence,
Silence,
Beauty,
Moments of stillness,
Breath.

The Art and Spirit of Leadership
judybrown@aol.com   www.judysorumbrown.com

I feel as if
I should be
doing more.

Perhaps
I should
be doing
less.

Judy Brown, January 10, 2009

What a funny phrase: " Perhaps I should be doing less," at the end
of all these pages and pages of words and notions, prose and
poetry. Less it is not. But it has been a gift for me. It has given
me space to experience calm, presence, silence, beauty, moments
of stillness, breath. I revel in the gift of the space of these words,
in the gift of poetry.

I invite you to join me in further reflection, to create space for
further learning, yours and mine. And to consider the trail on
which we find ourselves. And the practices that shape that trail.

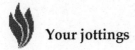 **Your jottings**

The Art and Spirit of Leadership
judybrown@aol.com   www.judysorumbrown.com

Trail

The words trail after
paths the heart makes,
rivulets the waters of
the mind carve
on the sandy shores
where rivers meet the sea,
where our lives meet the world.

The words trail after what we do,
the struggles that we live,
the demons that we own,
our questions and our truths.

The words trail after,
like paths worn down
by animals that moving
through the woods mark ways
between the trees,
not meaning to blaze
trails but simply leaving
them as they go on about their work,
paths that were there and always
but not evident to us
until small paws
we never saw
packed down the moss and leaves
to mark the way.

The Art and Spirit of Leadership
judybrown@aol.com   www.judysorumbrown.com

The words trail after
all the doing and the living,
to let us know where we have been,
to mark a space of journey
so that we can see our lives,
and so that others if they wish
who come thereafter, can
traverse the trail at least in part
knowing that someone
has been there before.

Thus they,
walking with easier stride than we could,
on a trail that's marked,
can travel further than we have.

And so the words
may be an after-thought
and yet a beacon to ourselves,
a compass built in traveling,
a generous light to glow
within the darks spots
of our lives, together.

Words of learning, joy, of loss, of clarity,
the words of vulnerability and grace,
words of confusion,
our humanity,
they mark the way.

The Art and Spirit of Leadership
judybrown@aol.com www.judysorumbrown.com

And even if the world
were never to have seen
the words, still they
would mark the places we have
traveled in our minds and hearts,
the spaces where we have
been present to the world
and to ourselves.

They honor actions which we took
or tried. They give
back gifts, gold held in trust,
ours only in the passing here.

So write down words.
Collect them.
Hold them close.
Squeeze out the moments
like a sponge. Find
solitude to give them space.

Write on old slips of paper,
backs of check stubs,
grocery lists.
Use toll receipts
and paper towels,
old envelopes.
Find scraps of time
and scraps of paper.

The Art and Spirit of Leadership
judybrown@aol.com   www.judysorumbrown.com

Fill up your heart
by emptying yourself
of words; be graced by
giving everything away.

Reveal your self and
heal yourself by your own
generosity of heart and mind.

Lay down the words
that are the trail
of life.

Judy Brown March 7, 1997

The Art and Spirit of Leadership
judybrown@aol.com   www.judysorumbrown.com

Bibliography

Alexander, Christopher, Ishikawa, Sara and Silverstein, Murray. (1977) *A Pattern Language.* Oxford Press.

Arbinger Institute. (2010) *Leadership and Self-Deception: Getting out of the Box.* Berrett-Koehler.

Bly, Robert. (1997) *Morning Poems.* Harper Collins.

Bridges, William. (2009) *Managing Transitions: Making the Most of Change.* Da Capo Press.

Bridges, William. (2004) *Transitions: Making Sense of Life's Changes.* Da Capo Press.

Bridges, William. (2001) *The Way of Transition.* Da Capo Press.

Brown, Judy. (1995) *The Choice: Seasons of Loss and Renewals after a Father's Decision to Die.* Conari Press.

Brown, Judy. (2000) *The Sea Accepts All Rivers and Other Poems.* Miles River Press. Available from the author.

Brown Judy. (2007) *A Leader's Guide to Reflective Practice.* Trafford Publishing.

Brown, Judy (2011) *Simple Gifts* Trafford Publishing

Buber, Martin. (2006) *I and Thou.* Hesperides.

Callaghan, Paul and Manhire, Bill, Editors. (2007) *Are Angels OK? The Parallel Universes of New Zealand Writers and Scientists.* Victoria University Press.

Center for Creative Leadership. (2003) *Visual Explorer.* Jossey-Bass.

Chopra, Deepak. (2004) *Spontaneous Fulfillment of Desire: Harnessing the Infinite Power of Coincidence.* Three River Press.

Collins, Billy. (2002) *Sailing around the Room: New and Selected Poems.* Random House.

Cooperrider, D.L. and D. Whitney. (1999) *Appreciative Inquiry.* Berrett-Koehler.

Dickenson, Emily. (1976) *The Complete Poems of Emily Dickenson.* Back Bay.

Einstein, Albert; Alice Calaprice, Editor. (2010) *The Ultimate Quotable Einstein.* Princeton University Press.

Franck, Frederick. (1973) *The Zen of Seeing: Seeing/Drawing as Meditation.* Vintage Books.

Franklin, Benjamin. (2011) *Autobiography.* Tribeca Books.

Frost, Robert. (1969) *The Poetry of Robert Frost: The Collected Poems Complete and Unabridged.* Henry Holt.

Gardner, John W. (1990) *On Leadership.* The Free Press.

Gardner, John W. Francesca Gardner, Editor. (2003) *Living, Leading, and the American Dream.* Jossey-Bass; A Wiley Imprint.

Gelb, Michael. (2000) *How to Think Like Leonardo Da Vinci.* Dell.

Giono, Jean. (2003) *The Man Who Planted Trees.* Random House; UK.

Gladwell, Malcolm. (2008) *Outliers: The Story of Success.* Little, Brown.

Graham, Martha. (2002) *Blood Memory: an Autobiography.* Washington Square Press.

Havel, Vaclav. (1989) *Letters to Olga.* Henry Holt.

Heifetz, Ronald A. (1994) *Leadership Without Easy Answers.* Cambridge, Massachusetts: Belknapp Press of Harvard University Press.

Heifetz, Ronald A. and Linsky, Marty. (2002) *Leadership on the Line: Staying Alive through the Dangers of Leading.* Boston, Massachusetts: Harvard Business School Press.

Heifetz, Ronald A., Linsky, Marty and Grashow, Alexander. (2009) *The Practice of Adaptive Leadership: Tools and Tactics for Changing Your Organization and the World.* Harvard Business Press.

Hott, Lawrence and Lewis, Tom, Directors. *Divided Highways.* Films for the Humanities.

Hughes, Langston. (1994) *The Collected Poems of Langston Hughes.* New York, New York: Alfred A. Knopf.

Hughes, Richard L., Ginnett, Robert C. and Curphy, Gordon J. (2011) *Leadership: Enhancing the Lessons of Experience.* McGraw-Hill.

Intrator, Sam M. and Megan Scribner, Editors. (2003) *Teaching with Fire: Poetry that Sustains the Courage to Teach.* Jossey-Bass.

Intrator, Sam M. and Megan Scribner, Editors. (2007) *Leading From Within: Poetry that Sustains the Courage to Lead.* Jossey-Bass.

Jones, Michael. (1995) *Creating an Imaginative Life.* Conari Press.

Keillor, Garrison, Editor. (2003) *Good Poems: Selected and Introduced by Garrison Keiller.* Penguin.

King, Martin Luther. "Letter from Birmingham City Jail." (Written to fellow clergymen in 1963). Christian Century. 80, June 12, 1963, 767-773.

King, Martin Luther. (1992) *I Have a Dream: Writings and Speeches that Changed the World.* Harperworld.

Kuhn, Thomas. (1996) *The Structure of Scientific Revolution.* University of Chicago Press.

Lengel, Robert and Daft, Richard. (2000) *Fusion Leadership.* Berrett-Koehler.

Losada, Marcial F. (1998) "The Complex Dynamics of High Performance Teams." *Mathematical and Computer Modeling.* Oxford, England: Elsevier Science.

Losada, Marcial F. and Heaphy, Emily. "The Role of Positivity and Connectivity in the Performance of Business Teams: A Nonlinear Dynamical Model." *American Behavioral Scientist.* (February 2004) Vol. 47, No 6, pp. 740-765.

Losada, Marcial and Fredrickson, Barbara. "Positive Affect and The Complex Dynamics of Human Flourishing." *American Psychologist.* (October 2005) pp. 678-686.

Maturana, Humberto and Varela, Francisco. (1992) *The Tree of Knowledge, The Biological Roots of Human Understanding.* Shambhala.

Merton, Thomas. (2010) *The Way of Chuang Tzu.* New Directions.

Milne, A.A. (1996) *The Complete Tales of Winnie-the-Pooh.* Dutton.

Mintzberg, Henry. (1987) "Crafting Strategy." *Harvard Business Review,* 65(4), 66-77.

Moon, Richard. (1996) *The Power of Harmony, Aikido in Three Easy Lessons.* Aiki Press.

Nepo, Mark. (2011) *The Book of Awakening.* Conari Press.

Oliver, Mary. (2005) *New and Selected Poems.* Beacon Press.

Palmer, Parker J. (1998) *The Courage to Teach.* Jossey-Bass.

Palmer, Parker J. (2000) *Let Your Life Speak: Listening for the Voice of Vocation.* Jossey-Bass.

Potts, Paul. (2007) *One Chance. DVD,* Sony.

Progoff, Ira. (1992) *At a Journal Workshop.* Tarcher.

Roosevelt, Eleanor. (2000) *Autobiography.* DaCapo Press.

Rumi. (1999) *Open Secret.,* Putney, Vermont: Threshold Books.

Scharmer, Otto. (2009) *Theory U: Leading from the Future as it Emerges.* Berrett-Koehler.

Scott, Susan. (2004) *Fierce Conversation: Achieving Success at Work & in Life, One Conversation at a Time.* Berkley.

Seligman, Martin. (2006) *Learned Optimism, How to Chang your Mind and your Life.* Vintage.

Senge, Peter, Scharmer, C. Otto, Jaworski, Joseph and Flowers, Betty Sue. (2004) *Presence: Human Purpose and the Field of the Future.* Cambridge, Massachusetts: The Society for Organizational Learning.

Senge, Peter M. (1990) *The Fifth Discipline.* Doubleday.

Senge, Peter M. (1994) *The Fifth Discipline Field Book.* Crown Business.

Shackleton, Ernest. (2002) *Shackleton's Antarctic Adventure.* Image
    Entertainment.

Spencer, Paula Underwood. (1983) *Who Speaks for Wolf.* Austin: Tribe of
    Two Press.

Stafford, William. (1999) *The Way it Is.* Graywolf Press.

Thurber, James. (1999) *The Thurber Carnival.* Harper.

Underwood, Paula. (1994) *Three Strands in the Braid: A Guide for Enablers
    of Learning.* A Tribe of Two Press.

Walcott, Derek. (1987) *Collected Poems 1948-1984.* Farrar, Straus and
    Giroux.

Wainwright, Alfred. (2003) *A Coast to Coast Walk.* Frances Lincoln.

Zander, Rosamund Stone and Benjamin. (2002) *The Art of Possibility:
    Transforming Professional and Personal Life.* Penguin.